Amazing Grace for Married Couples

Amazing Grace
for Married Couples

12 Life-Changing Stories
of Renewed Love

Edited by
Jeff Cavins, Matthew Pinto and
Patti Maguire Armstrong

ASCENSION
PRESS

West Chester, Pennsylvania

Ascension Press
Post Office Box 1990
West Chester, PA 19380
Orders: 1-800-376-0520
www.AscensionPress.com

Cover design: Kinsey Caruth

Printed in the United States of America
11 8 7 6 5 4 3

ISBN 978-1-932645-79-8

In thanksgiving to Pope John Paul II for his extraordinary teachings on love and marriage, and for our spouses, Emily Cavins, Maryanne Pinto, and Mark Armstrong.

— Jeff Cavins, Matthew Pinto and
Patti Maguire Armstrong

Contents

Introduction

Marriage is not for the faint of heart. It is often likened to heaven or hell and everything in between. This covenant made on the wings of romantic love usually begins with a physical or emotional attraction. If love takes root and grows under God's care, it will flourish and blossom; if not, it can easily wither and die.

The marital union is meant to last a lifetime—in sickness and in health, in good times and bad. It is a contract made between a man and woman and sealed by God. "What therefore God has joined together, let no man put asunder" (Matthew 19:6). Yet, when we say "I do," who really knows the true immensity of that commitment? No amount of marriage preparation, sage advice, or witnessing failed marriages firsthand can adequately prepare us for bad times or difficult situations.

Because we are human, our emotions are often transitory. The rush of "being in love" colors everything, especially how we see our partner. Once the infatuation fades, though, we often feel disillusioned or regretful about our life choice. Without turning to God and drawing on His grace, we could easily begin down the path that leads to divorce. But, by rising above the obstacles, true love can grow and replace mere infatuation.

The marriages of the couples recounted in this book all began with the confidence that they were lasting unions. Some of these couples were cautious about getting married, making sure that their partner was "the one." These men and women did not just jump into marriage but considered all the qualities they were looking for in a lifetime mate. Others acted more impulsively and failed to fully consider the magnitude of such a decision. Regardless of their perceived readiness to marry, these couples all ended up experiencing profound marital crises. In some cases, their marriages fell apart very quickly, while others experienced many years of happiness before things unraveled. Either way, all their stories provide us with two clear messages: 1) There are no guarantees for a happy marriage; and 2) There are no marital problems too big for God to handle.

While not every married couple will go through the extreme levels of turmoil and stress as the couples in this book, this actually makes their stories especially relevant to everyone. For if your marital problems are less severe—more "ordinary"—then you can take comfort in the knowledge that, if these couples could overcome their seemingly insurmountable problems, you can overcome your more "minor" issues. On the other hand, if you suffer a greater degree of difficulty, these stories will show you that you are not alone and that God has grace enough for you, too.

The couples chronicled here were eventually humbled by the realization that if they had ended their marriages, they would have missed out on a love deeper than they ever imagined possible. One of the husbands who shares his journey in this book came to realize that, regardless of his wife's response, he was married "until death do us part" and that unconditional love is necessary even if a wayward spouse never changes. This unconditional love requires us to love our spouse as ourselves and be willing to suffer for that love.

It must be said, though, that no one is forced to remain in a situation that involves physical abuse. Sometimes couples must separate for their own safety and that of their children. Such a separation, though, is always undertaken with the hope of healing and reconciliation.

Only after we have experienced marriage can we understand the challenge of maintaining a strong, loving union through good times and bad. It is then that we come to understand the role God plays in our married life. For marriage is not merely a covenant between two people, but between three: husband, wife, and God. It is God who helps us do what at times seems difficult, even impossible—to keep our marriage promises to love and honor our spouse all the days of our life.

This book is a celebration of those promises. Each story is a type of resurrection: love that died was born again. Just as the resurrection of Christ gives us hope of eternal life, so these inspiring stories of renewed love give us hope that with God's help, we can overcome all obstacles. So whatever the state of your union, however long you have been married—or have been planning your wedding—we hope that these stories will inspire you to deepen your own bond of love through God's amazing grace.

—Jeff Cavins, Matthew Pinto, and
Patti Maguire Armstrong

1
Through Fire

"I want a divorce," my husband blurted out. My heart dropped to the pit of my stomach and I began to shake. For the better part of our twenty-five years of marriage, I lived in constant fear of hearing those words. It was not the first time I had heard them.

When Rusty and I married, I was eighteen and he was twenty-five. It was 1965, and I became pregnant during my senior year in high school. I was married in March, graduated in June, and had a baby girl in October; an eventful year, to be sure. Although an out-of-wedlock pregnancy was still considered a scandal in the mid-1960s, I was thrilled.

At this time in my life, having a baby filled me with hope for a happier future. My mother had died when I was only eight years old. By the time I was seventeen, my stepsister, who was also my best friend, had died in an accident. My stepmother left my dad, and he ended up in a mental institution. I was living with friends and felt I had no family of my own. Getting married and becoming a mother seemed like the best thing I could hope for. "I will have a family and a husband to take care of me," I had thought. I was completely unaware that Rusty felt trapped. Back then, when a guy got his girlfriend pregnant, he married her, plain and simple.

Rusty was very driven to be a millionaire by the time he was thirty. After we married, he started his own business as a contractor and buried himself in work. Within six years I had five pregnancies but lost one to miscarriage and two to stillbirth. It seemed that loss through death followed me everywhere. But I had been blessed with a little girl, Nikki, and a baby boy, Todd. I loved being a mom and would have had eight children if it were up to me. Rusty seemed willing to go along with whatever I wanted to do, so he allowed me to take in foster children.

As much as I loved mothering children, I also longed for my husband to cherish me. Rusty and I communicated very little. He was a great provider but worked long hours and only had dinner with us about once a week. By the time I was twenty-four, my loneliness led me to God. I joined a women's Bible study and found a relationship with Jesus to comfort me.

When I was twenty-six, my older sister committed suicide. Two weeks later my father-in-law, whom I had grown very close to, also died. Although I had experienced death so many times, I grieved these losses deeply. Then, within a few months, my heart felt it had been ripped apart as Rusty confessed he was having an affair and wanted a divorce.

Given my life, I would not have been as shocked if death had taken Rusty from me. It was the way my loved ones kept leaving me. But another woman was not what I imagined would end my marriage.

"Please don't leave me," I had cried. I had a strong faith but no self-esteem. I believed that if I could just do better—be a better wife, lose more weight, become more interesting—that my husband would not want to leave me. Since it was shortly before Christmas, we agreed that Rusty would not leave until after the holidays. Our children were only nine and six. I was desperate to keep Rusty and grateful for a couple of weeks to try and win him back. When the holidays were over, however, Rusty left. He was only gone for two weeks before returning out of guilt.

Even though I knew Rusty was back only out of a sense of obligation, I convinced myself that I could become a better person so he would not want anyone else. I read self-help books and did everything I could think of to make him happy. I also threw myself into the job of motherhood. There was nothing I would not do for my husband or my beloved children.

Although work filled Rusty's life, we still took annual vacations alone with each other and then another vacation with the kids. Our conversations were always very superficial, but I convinced myself that things would be OK. I also prayed for Rusty to become a Christian. The children attended Christian schools, and they went to church on Sundays with me. Rusty knew I wanted him to come with us, but I never nagged him about it. I knew I could not force Jesus on him, but I sure prayed that one day he would seek out faith on his own.

Then, in my thirties, Rusty again had an affair and told me he wanted a divorce. Again, it blew over and he returned. And again, I kept trying harder to be a better wife. As the kids became teenagers, they began to resent Rusty's lack of involvement and rebelled. Our son, Todd, got involved with drugs and became a crack addict. It was a wake-up call for Rusty. Todd needed drug rehabilitation, and we feared for his life. "I'm not doing one more thing for the children without you," I informed Rusty. I demanded that either both of us would be involved in Todd's drug counseling or no one would. Rusty agreed. It was the first time the two of us really communicated and worked together. It felt so good to work as a team. Our son entered inpatient treatment and made a commitment to stay drug free. Not long after, he joined the army.

As our twenty-fifth wedding anniversary approached, I thought to myself, *We've made it.* Our daughter was in college, and our son was now doing well. After all these years and close calls, Rusty and I were still together. To celebrate, we went on a vacation to Hawaii.

It was not surprising that there would be a lot of phone calls from Rusty's business while we were away. That was typical. But something in the pit of my stomach told me that some of the calls were not just business. *Is there another woman?* I wondered. I tried to push the thought out of my mind. *We've come so far,* I convinced myself.

Shortly after we returned from Hawaii, Rusty confessed. There was indeed another woman. Rusty again wanted out of the marriage. I looked at him—the man whose love I had fought so hard for so many years—and I finally gave up. "All right," I sighed. "Do what you need to do." I was tired of fighting for him.

That evening, I sat in front of my house with Christian music playing and the floodlights on. I looked at the four flats of flowers waiting to be planted. Tears rolled down my cheeks. When I was a child, I had an aunt who told me that if you had lots of flowers outside your home, it meant you had a happy home. I had the flowers but happiness eluded me.

At the age of forty-four, I was alone for the first time in my life. I had learned in my early twenties that I needed to depend on the Lord instead of my husband. Through the years of workaholism and unfaithfulness, I had prayed daily for guidance and wisdom for our family. No matter how hard I tried, I could not change Rusty; I could only change myself. Psalm 37:4 had been my guide. "Take delight in the Lord, and he will give you the desires of your heart." My desires were to have a family and husband that loved and adored me.

As I sat in the dirt, crying, peace came over me. My faith in God was rock solid. It suddenly occurred to me that I could always depend on the Lord. *Lord, I tried my hardest, but Rusty's leaving is not about me, is it?* I prayed. *I know you have a plan for my life and I realize it might not include him.*

I began building a life without Rusty and discovered that it was a relief, at times even a joy. After years of taking care of everyone else, it was just the Lord and me. I still prayed for my husband every day, but I realized he had to find his own way. I joined a Christian singles group, attended a divorce recovery workshop, and took college classes.

Six months after he left, Rusty called. He wanted to see me. After returning from a six-week backpacking trip in Australia with our son, he announced he had accepted the Lord into his life. With tears in his eyes, Rusty told me he no longer wanted a divorce but instead wanted to work on our marriage. I looked at him and did not speak for a moment. My life was good now. I was more content than I had ever been. After so many years of living in crisis, I had discovered how nice it was to live without it. *Would I return to a life of deception?* I wondered. *Was Rusty deceiving me now just to get me back?* The divorce papers were already signed and the legal procedures were just waiting to be finalized. I was angry that he had already stopped the process without consulting me.

"I need time to think about this," I informed him. I spent the next few days in prayer. The psalm had said the Lord would give me the desires of my heart. I had prayed for my husband for twenty-five years to come to know the Lord. I did not trust my husband, but I did trust God. I felt God saying: "You can doubt him all day long, but do you doubt me? You've prayed to me for all these years, and now are you saying you don't want to work on this marriage?" I realized my prayers were being answered, so now was not the time to give up.

I agreed to work on the marriage, but with a list of conditions. "If you think you can live with these boundaries, I will work with you," I agreed, half-expecting Rusty to decide it was too much. I insisted that we both see a Christian counselor once a week as well as going to weekly counseling as a couple. "While we work on our relationship, don't even think about spending the night here or kissing me," I informed him. "There will be no sexual contact during this time. If you know the Lord, you'll want to know my new friends who love the Lord, too. I also expect you'll want to attend church on Sundays if your love for God is real," I continued. "And the other woman has to be completely out of the picture." I ended my list with one last demand: "If this turns out to be God's work, I want a wedding. I want the gown, the church, and for you to wear a ring." Rusty never wanted a ring, so I had never given him one. To my surprise, he agreed to everything.

After all my years of energy, it seemed I had little left to invest in the marriage now. My attitude was that if Rusty wanted to stay married, then he could do all the work because I did the first twenty-five years of work by myself. I almost think I was trying to sabotage him. I truly thought I had set up an impossible scenario.

To my surprise, Rusty met all my conditions and worked very hard. When he sold his business so he could pour all his energy into our marriage, I became convinced of his sincerity. It was his work that he had really been married to all those years.

As the months went by, God did the work of mending our very broken relationship. Rusty and I got to know each other like never before. Christ became the center of our relationship, and we really fell in love for the first time. On our twenty-sixth wedding anniversary, with friends and family in attendance, Rusty and I renewed our marriage vows. Our drug-free son walked me down the aisle to meet a completely transformed man. Our beautiful daughter sang, "Let's Begin Again." We did begin again. My childhood dreams came true. I was married to a man who cherished me and worked hard to prove his love for me. He had become the man of my dreams. I was forty-five and Rusty was fifty-two.

We honeymooned in the Cayman Islands and behaved like newlyweds. Later, Rusty took me to Australia where we backpacked together. Life was good beyond my wildest imagination until two-and-a-half years after our second wedding. It was Saturday night, August 28, 1993. We were traveling with our daughter, Nikki, in our motor home on Interstate 55 near Corning, California, on our way to Washington state.

I was jolted awake from the back of the motor home and thrown across the vehicle. We had been in an accident and our gas tank was punctured. I was asleep in the back. In a flash, a wall of flames went up between me and Rusty, who was driving, and our twenty-seven-year-old daughter in the passenger seat.

The fire was impenetrable, but I was able to kick my way through a hole ripped into the side of the motor home. Although my skin was not on fire, it was scorched. Blood ran into my eyes, dripping from my forehead. Escaping from the motor home provided no relief. Flames enveloped me in the gully where I landed. The grass was on fire. I attempted to flee by climbing a wire fence along the highway, but fell back. From across the fence, two men reached over to save me.

My only thought was for my family. Thick black smoke hid the motor home from my view. "Save my family!" I frantically screamed. Yet I could not imagine that they could still be alive. As I lay waiting for medical help to arrive, a policeman gently told me: "Your family is up the road. They're alive."

"Thank God," I thought and then prayed. "Please help us!" Every inch of my body was flooded with pain. When medical help arrived and Rusty was taken first, I knew he had to be in the worst condition. We were all taken to Chico Hospital to be stabilized, but Rusty was transported by helicopter to the burn unit at UC–Davis Medical Center in Sacramento.

My burned flesh began swelling, so the emergency room nurse needed to cut my wedding ring off. It felt like she was cutting my heart. That ring had so recently become a symbol of the deep love Rusty and I shared as man and wife. *Now what?* I wondered and cried.

The helicopter that had transported Rusty returned for me. Thankfully, Nikki was not burned, but her back and arm were broken and her knees were dislocated. As I was wheeled out, I heard Nikki crying for me. I ached to hold her, but I could not move nor even call out to her.

By the time I arrived at the burn unit, close friends and relatives were there. They informed me that a prayer vigil on our behalf had already begun. *Lord, I know you will see us through*, I thought. But this was to be the fight of our lives. We never needed God more. My back was broken and forty-eight percent of my body was burned. Rusty, who was just down the hall from me, was only semiconscious. He had burns on over sixty-eight percent of his body, and he had been given only a nine percent chance of survival.

For me, not even strong pain medication could soothe the unbearable pain. Skin grafts and bandage changes did what seemed impossible—they actually increased the pain. Although I hung onto my faith, it felt like not even Jesus could lift me from the deep depression that enveloped me. My intolerable existence made each minute crawl by, day after day, week after week, until summer slipped into fall. Friends and family visited and then walked away to their pain-free lives. *Oh, to walk out that door,* I thought. The reassurances that at least we were all alive felt hollow. Living did not seem like the better option sometimes.

But I always knew God was with me. Friends and family reminded me constantly of all the prayers being said for me and Rusty. Worship and praise songs kept me company, especially through bandage changes and painful procedures. During rehab, I said a Bible verse over and over: "I can do all things in [Christ] who strengthens me" (Phil 4:13.)

And always, I prayed and talked with God. I prayed especially for Rusty. He needed a miracle to survive.

I did not want to live without Rusty, but I realized the odds were not in his favor. He was in my heart and prayers each day, but I could not bring myself to see him. The thought of seeing my beloved husband swollen, bandaged, and hooked to machines was overwhelming. Instead, I taped messages for him, hoping my voice would break through his coma. While I spoke messages of love into the microphone, I imagined looking into the face of the Rusty of our youth.

On October 3, 1993, six weeks after the accident, my niece, Vicki, brought me home from the hospital. She had moved into our house to care for me around the clock for the next five months. Many friends and family visited Rusty regularly in the hospital, but I had left without seeing him. I just couldn't bear it. Just knowing the extent of his suffering added a heavy burden to my own. I did not feel strong enough to see Rusty under the circumstances.

Twelve days after I left the hospital, Rusty nearly died. When he pulled through later that day, doctors became more confident that he was going to make it. It was time for me to see him. Our friend, Don, wheeled me beside Rusty's bed while he slept. I looked at my beloved husband and longed to hold his broken body. His face was fractured and swollen beyond recognition with his left ear partially burned away and his left eye destroyed. Since Rusty was still only semiconscious, the doctors were not sure if he had suffered any brain damage. Although it pained me to see Rusty in such terrible condition, I felt peace surrounding him. God was with us.

Rusty returned home three days before Christmas. We slept in separate bedrooms because of the pain, and each of us needed to concentrate on our own rehabilitation. I missed the closeness we had enjoyed before the accident. My injuries were less severe and I had made some progress towards recovery, so when Rusty struggled to find the will to go on, I was able to encourage him. By the grace of God I found the words to help him make the transition from victim to survivor.

It was our own Calvary, our own Cross. The struggles were monumental and the pain intense. Weariness nipped at our heels at every turn. But just as God had healed us spiritually and renewed our marriage, He was now healing us physically and emotionally. We prayed continuously and daily felt the healing power of God.

Twelve years have passed since the accident. My physical abilities are nearly what they were before, although I do have some limitations due to my back injury. Rusty has had many operations and plastic surgeries. He recently obtained a lens which improves his vision enough so that he can read and work again—something he was unable to do for years. Even with amputated fingers on his left hand and a prosthetic eye, he lives a productive life each day. Our daughter, Nikki, has had both physical and emotional struggles, but healing is a gradual process.

There is a type of pine cone that only opens and sheds its seeds when it encounters the intense heat of a forest fire. It is God's amazing way of insuring that, after a fire, there will be new life. For Rusty and me, the fire allowed the seeds of our renewed love to take root and grow stronger than the biggest tree in the forest. We were tested by fire and strengthened through Christ. Our love for each other has never been deeper. Even our once-broken family has come together in new life. We live together now on a farm with our adult children and their families. The young lives of our five grandchildren fills us with a love of life, a love for each other and a deep love for God.

So many people have told me that our story has given them strength to overcome their struggles. I now work with burn survivors and their families to help them through the long recovery of healing. My ministry is called "Rays'd Up." Look beneath the surface, rise up in dignity and value, burst through to new life. "Goodness will shine on you like the sun, with healing in its rays" (Mal 4:2). God truly can use all things for good.

–Susan Lugli

Susan Lugli *has stories published in eight books, including three in the* Chicken Soup *series. She is a public speaker and an active member of the Phoenix Society for Burn Survivors. Susan and Rusty live on a ranch in California with their family. Her website is www.susanlugli.com.*

2

God and Dustin to the Rescue

"Your baby's measurements do not seem quite right," the doctor explained to Liz Gary, who was seven months pregnant with her third baby. The doctor's words were calm and carefully chosen; a professional all the way. "It also appears that he might have a heart defect and possibly some fluid on the lungs. We will need to do more testing."

Liz began shaking. *No!* her thoughts screamed. *I couldn't handle that!* Life already seemed so unbearable. Her marriage to Mike felt dead and the tasks of motherhood had become terribly burdensome. Now she cringed at the realization that her deepest fear might come to pass—to have a child with a disability like Down Syndrome.

After scheduling an amniocentesis, Liz left the doctor's office numb with fear. "How will I manage?" she cried as she drove home. Turning to Mike when he got home from work brought Liz no relief. It had become so hard for her to communicate with him. Mike seemed immune to her unhappiness. Problems were never solved and his typical response was to tune her complaints out. Mike's reaction to the news angered Liz. "We'll get through this," he had said. "Everything will be OK."

Liz wanted to scream at him to wake up and get real. She was tired of his outward calm and impenetrable emotions. How could he say that everything would be OK? Nothing was OK! Things had not been OK for a very long time. Liz so desperately wanted the happily-ever-after she thought they were assured of on their wedding day. She wanted to be in love with Mike again, but that seemed only a distant memory now.

When Liz had strolled into her statistics class at the University of New Orleans in the winter of 1989, her heart skipped a beat as her eyes rested on a handsome redhead. He was talking with a group of her friends. Although Liz was not given to girlish notions, she was suddenly overcome with the thought that this was the man she would marry.

Liz approached the group slowly and smiled at everyone. Casual introductions were made before class commenced. But Mike had something other than statistics on his mind. *Those are the most beautiful eyes I've ever seen*, he thought, giving Liz sidelong glances. Mike's thoughts had not made as big a leap as Liz's, but she definitely had his attention.

After class, when Mike discovered that a good friend of his was hoping to date Liz, he bowed out. Liz was disappointed that Mike did not seem to return her interest. Then, one evening, he called to ask her a question about statistics. The call lasted more than an hour. Once Mike realized that Liz and his friend would not be dating, he carefully made his move. Not wanting to seem overanxious, he asked Liz if she wanted to get together to study. Of course, she said yes.

The relationship proceeded slowly. Mike was cautious but he was definitely smitten. His cool exterior made Liz wonder until one afternoon she received a delivery of a dozen, long-stemmed red roses. "Happy Birthday from Mike" the card read. The warm tingle of love rushed through her— yes this was the man she wanted to marry.

By May, Mike and Liz had shifted easily into an exclusive dating relationship. Mike's natural shyness evaporated around Liz. He enjoyed her lively, outgoing personality and she appreciated his calm, easy-going demeanor. That Christmas, Liz opened a small box that held a sapphire ring.

"It's beautiful," she gushed. But inwardly she wondered: *What does this mean? Are we engaged? Nothing has ever been said.* Mike loved Liz and he was as certain as she was that they were made for each other. But Mike was not one to communicate his feelings. He assumed that his actions said it all.

The next Christmas when Mike gave Liz a hope chest, she again wondered just how serious he was. And Mike again assumed that the gift said it all; what need was there to spell it out? *After all, you don't give a hope chest to a girl unless you are planning on marrying her,* he concluded.

Liz loved Mike with all her heart. She had no interest in dating other men, but she did not want to appear to be pushing him into marriage. Yet, after two-and-a-half years of dating, she needed to know if Mike planned on marrying her. One evening at a friend's wedding, she felt she got her answer. It was not what she had hoped for. When someone asked Mike about marriage, he coyly responded that he did not know when or if they would ever marry.

Mike's casual remark cut through Liz's heart. That night, a flood of tears soaked her pillow, but by morning, she determined the relationship needed to end. Enough was enough. If Mike did not plan to marry her, then she needed to get on with her life. When Mike called that day to ask her to join him for Sunday dinner at his parent's house, Liz told him the relationship was over.

Liz's rejection caught Mike off guard and forced him to reveal a surprise he was planning. The day before, he had put money down on an engagement ring. Liz's tears suddenly became tears of joy. Mike really did love her as much as she loved him.

When Mike and Liz walked down the aisle on November 13, 1992, they felt certain that this was not just "forever" but also "happily ever after." If there was such a thing as "love at first sight," they had been hit with it. Yet their relationship was not impulsive. They both were out of college, working at good jobs, and had known each other for almost three years. Their future seemed secure.

Liz worked at United Parcel Service and Mike worked for Federal Express. Shortly after the wedding, Liz received a huge promotion with a big salary attached. There would be some traveling and long hours, but it was a big opportunity. Liz felt that she could either give 100 percent to a job or 100 percent to her family. She could not do both. The realization of what this job would demand was overwhelming. Having a family was a priority for Liz, not climbing the corporate ladder.

Mike's easygoing, understanding nature came through. He admitted the extra money would have been nice, but Liz's happiness was more important to him. Liz took a lower-level position, and she and Mike enjoyed a couple years as newlyweds—a relatively carefree life just enjoying each other's company.

Three years after getting married, their daughter Abby-Lynn was born. Mike and Liz slid happily into the role of new parents. Liz found a job close to home at a pre-school to which she could bring her daughter with her to work. Surely, this was the "happily ever after." Liz loved being a mom so much, and she truly wanted two more children. Although Mike was easygoing on most issues, he was adamant that they would only have two children. He was worried about the money and thought two children would be all they could handle.

Once their son, Cameron, was born two-and-a-half years later, Mike felt they had the perfect family—a boy and a girl. Shortly after the second baby, Liz's own dream of having a third child soon vanished under the stress of caring for a difficult baby.

Cameron squirmed and cried inconsolably. "He's just a fussy baby," the doctors repeatedly said. But as the months passed and Cameron continued to appear to be in constant distress, Liz's instincts told her something else was going on. She took him to several doctors and spent hours on the Internet searching for answers to Cameron's symptoms.

Stress and lack of sleep due to Cameron turned Liz into a shell of her former self. Struggling through days of zombie-like fatigue to care for a perpetually unhappy baby drove her to tears. "Something is wrong with him," Liz insisted repeatedly. Mike would shrug and remind her that the doctors said some babies are just fussy.

As the heavy load of mothering consumed her, Liz began to resent Mike. She believed that Mike should be helping more around the house and be more sympathetic to her situation. When she complained, he tended to tune her out. Mike avoided communicating with Liz at this time because it felt to him like she always wanted to vent her frustration and blame him for things. It was a vicious cycle that began eating away at Liz.

From Mike's perspective, he expected there would be good times and bad in their marriage. These were just some of the difficult times. He supposed it to be a phase that would eventually turn itself around. Mike did not want to fight, so he decided that the best thing to do was to avoid confrontations, which meant he avoided any real communication with Liz.

Liz did not view the situation so lightly. Her life felt empty, stressful, and monotonous. The one thing she had always wanted was a family. Yet it felt like her family was destroying her. As much as she wanted to love and care for Cameron, he seemed miserable. It made her feel guilty that she could not help him. Liz also felt guilty that Abby-Lynn was not getting enough attention. And her husband just seemed to tune her out and make light of everything. Liz equated Mike's lack of understanding with a lack of caring.

Not only was their communication with each other strained, but Liz and Mike also did not have much of a relationship with God at this time. They attended Mass on Sundays and that was about it. God was not at the center of their family. He was thought about briefly on Sundays and then forgotten the rest of the week.

Just before Cameron turned two, Liz discovered she was pregnant again. Her heart sank when the home pregnancy test read positive. *How can I get through this?* she wondered. *I don't think I can handle another baby.*

At nine weeks, when there was no heart beat, an unexpected emptiness reverberated through her. *My baby is gone,* Liz realized. *But I guess it's for the best,* she decided. *I don't think I could have handled it.* Yet when she actually miscarried and held the tiny nine-week old baby in her hands, Mike and Liz both cried. It was their own precious daughter; her soul gone to heaven. They were in awe that their tiny child was already so well-formed with little feet and hands. They named her June—the month she died. It was a gentle sadness that covered them because after all, they concluded, surely this baby was not meant to be a part of their chaotic lives.

A few months after the miscarriage, Liz found a doctor who discovered Cameron was suffering from high mercury levels due in large part to the series of hepatitis B vaccines he received as an infant. When the doctor began treatment and adjusted Cameron's diet, within days there were dramatic changes. The piercing screams, chronic diarrhea, and respiratory problems quickly faded. Cameron calmed down and began to smile.

For Liz, the relief was incredible. She could finally hug her baby with joy and not go through the day dreading his cries. The key to unlocking her son's misery had come at a steep financial cost, however. Liz was no longer bringing in a second income and the doctor bills had quickly mounted. Their savings account, which had once represented a secure future, was depleted. Financial strain added still more stress to the marriage.

Liz and Mike never spent time with just each other anymore either. They would occasionally say, "I love you" but it seemed to be nothing more than a habit. It was if they were merely roommates who did not seem to enjoy one another's company. Sometimes, Liz thought that picking up and leaving with the two kids would be the best solution. But she knew she would never have the guts to go through with such a plan. Liz told herself she just needed to face the fact that the magic was gone and accept the relationship for what it was.

Around Christmas of 2001, Liz again had a positive home pregnancy test. *Not again*, she thought, feeling sick. Cameron was three and Abby-Lynn was five. Liz braced herself for a negative reaction from Mike. Instead, he said he had already figured out that she was pregnant. Mike was determined to take life in stride and decided there was no point in worrying about it. Still, Liz was miserable. She felt her existence was empty and burdensome with no personal satisfaction. Another baby would mean more stress, more work, less sleep, and more strain on the marriage. Yet there was nothing to do but go forward, one monotonous day after another.

So, when Liz learned at seven months that her baby might be born with Down Syndrome, she could not accept it. Despair had left her feeling used up and empty inside. She wondered, *Where will I find the strength to cope?*

In reality, Mike also was reeling from the shock. He had no experience with anyone with Downs. He wondered, *What will this mean to my family and how will we manage?* Mike never doubted his love for Liz or their marriage. He accepted that Liz tended to be emotional and seemed negative much of the time. Mike chalked it up to her disposition and accepted it. While his nonchalant reaction to the news angered Liz, Mike was actually putting up a front in order to be strong for her.

Two days later, Mike accompanied Liz for the amniocentesis. It was during this procedure that Liz's life began to change. Laying on the surgical table, Liz realized the need to put herself in God's hands. The helpless, paralyzing fear that had overwhelmed her suddenly lifted. A gentle serenity filled her as if she was floating in God's hands. That feeling stayed with Liz for the next week. It was so profound and so real that people commented on how peaceful she seemed. For Liz, it was the beginning of a peace she had never known—acceptance that God is the one who controls our lives. Instead of fighting it, she accepted her own lack of control and began to look to God for everything.

But before the results of the amnio came back, Liz and her mother had convinced themselves that the baby did not have Downs. They had prayed and seen numerous things as signs that the baby did not have this syndrome. Liz was with her mother at the doctor's office when the results came back. Both became very emotional when Down Syndrome was confirmed.

When Liz told Mike of the confirmed diagnosis and he remained calm, it confused her. *Why isn't he upset?* she wondered. Although, in part, Mike was trying to hide his own fear, the words of a co-worker had also given him strength during this time. While everyone else had offered condolences and said things like "I'm so sorry," a man who was unable to have children of his own had reacted almost indifferently to the news. "So what?" he had said and shrugged. "You are going to love this child just as much as your other children."

The co-worker's matter-of-fact manner about a situation others saw as a tragedy somehow made everything seem so manageable. Mike realized that a baby, even with Down Syndrome, would be seen as a gift to his co-worker. Suddenly, Mike stopped viewing the baby as a burden and began seeing it as his son whom he would love.

Even though Liz's peace was shattered when forced to face the reality of her baby's condition, she continued to pray for strength. She also prayed that God would just take her innocent baby to heaven. She did not think she was capable of taking care of this child. On the subsequent doctor's appointment, it seemed that her prayer was being answered.

With Mike at her side, Liz lay on the table during an ultrasound. The doctor that examined the screen had grim news: the baby would not survive. At thirty-one weeks, he was swelling with fluid in major organs, a medical disorder called "non-immune hydrops." This condition was usually fatal.

Liz and Mike had opposite reactions. Liz was quietly relieved. It was what she had prayed for. But Mike broke down, sobbing. The words of his co-worker had come to pass; Mike truly loved this child like his others. Yet the grief that stabbed at his heart was completely unexpected. Earlier, he too had thought it would be best if the baby did not survive. But as he looked at the little heart beating on the monitor, the love Mike felt for his unborn son caught him by surprise. *That's my son*, he thought, *and he's going to die.*

Although Liz and Mike had different reactions to the diagnosis, they were one in their response to the doctor's recommendation that the baby be aborted. "We need to take him now," the doctor insisted. "Even if he survives the pregnancy—which is highly unlikely—he will not be able to live outside the womb. There's no reason to put yourself through all this. You should end it now."

But the experience of Liz holding June, their nine-week-old miscarried baby, solidified their view that life was precious at every stage. It was unthinkable that they would stop their own son's heart from beating. The doctor could not understand what she perceived to be an irrational decision. But Mike and Liz were resolved. They named their baby Dustin and put him in God's hands.

Liz gave up her natural inclination of wanting to be in control and made a complete surrender to God. *Your will be done*, she prayed. She asked for a miracle but she also told God she would accept whatever His will was. Mike and Liz began praying together like never before. Every night Mike and Liz joined with their kids and prayed for a miracle— and also for acceptance of whatever God deemed best.

When Liz left the hospital on the day of Dustin's grim prognosis, she went home to wait for him to die. Sometimes, sitting or lying down, she put her hand over her belly and felt Dustin moving in her womb. After a week of feeling his lively kicks and turns, she thought to herself, *This baby is acting like he's fighting to live.* As she experienced his life inside her, Liz's own emotions surprised her. She grew to love this baby with all her heart. Suddenly, she desperately wanted him no matter what. Liz agonized over her earlier plea for God to take her son to heaven. The realization that she was getting what she had wanted filled her with grief. *My shallow faith hindered my love for God and even for my own baby,* she mourned. *I'm so sorry, God,* Liz prayed. *Now, I put all my trust in You. Help me to trust and help my love to grow.*

Another thing that happened during this time was that Liz turned to Mike with all her emotions and Mike did not turn away. Their fear united them while their faith and trust in both God and each other grew. Every day Liz needed to hear Mike's voice and have him hold her. They learned how much they needed each other. Both strove to be strong for each other and for their children.

Although Mike tended to avoid emotional situations, he now reached out to Liz with his own emotions. No one else could understand what he was experiencing except Liz. While falling in love with their unborn son, Mike and Liz were falling in love with each other all over again.

Mike had always been the strong one for Liz, but she found herself wanting to protect him now. Plans had been made to have Dustin buried next to Mike's father, who had died a year before their wedding. Liz wanted to make the final arrangements ahead of time to spare Mike the pain. After visiting with a funeral director, Liz attempted to get the heartbreaking business of choosing a coffin out of the way. The director refused to allow it. "The baby is not dead yet," he gently told Liz. "I'm going to pray with you for a miracle and that I will never see you again."

The love and prayers of so many people began to reach their lives and touch Mike and Liz deeply. They were amazed to hear that people they did not even know were praying for them.

By the time Liz went into labor, there was a bond between her and Mike that transcended this world. They prepared as best as they could to surrender their child back to God. The new baby clothes packed in Liz's overnight bag were to be their son's funeral clothes. They cried and held each other as Liz's contractions heralded the end of Dustin's life. At the hospital, Liz had been put in the end room to keep her away from the other delivery rooms. The instruction to medical personnel was to make the baby comfortable until he passed. When the doctor told Liz it was time to push, she resisted because she knew that saying hello would also be saying good-bye.

Dustin Raphael Gary, a hearty seven pounds, ten ounces, was born alive, kicking and screaming. When Mike saw his little son, a new flood of tears burst forth. He had expected to see a blue and swollen baby but instead, the baby was pink and looked so normal. Love and grief, greater than he had ever known, poured from Mike as he looked on the little son he had been told was destined to die. Once the umbilical cord was cut, Liz and Mike frantically held their baby. With tears still falling down his cheeks, Mike quickly baptized Dustin. Liz and Mike told Dustin how much they loved him. They had but minutes to pour a lifetime of love into their son.

Within about ten minutes there was a gurgling sound. *This is it,* Mike and Liz both thought. A nurse syringed Dustin's throat and he opened his eyes and started rooting around to eat. *Please don't take him from me,* Liz pleaded with God. *I love him so much!*

Nurses started coming in and out of the room, not saying anything but seemingly surprised that it was taking Dustin so long to die. After about forty minutes, a nurse came in and said she was going to call a pediatrician. The doctor called for Dustin's charts and then examined him. With a confused look on his face, the doctor announced: "This is not the same baby." But it was.

Throughout the next two days, a number of doctors examined the charts and examined Dustin. Over and over again, the joyful couple heard: "This cannot be the same baby." Dustin did have Down Syndrome, but the non-immune hydrops which had caused swelling throughout his entire body had all but disappeared. There was only a very slight amount of fluid remaining.

No one could figure out what had happened. God had healed him and medical science had no explanation for it. The most painful day of Mike and Liz's lives turned out to be the happiest. Never had Mike and Liz felt so blessed. God had given them a miracle and, together, Dustin and God changed them.

Liz and Mike agreed that, through Dustin, they experienced God's love and life like never before. "Our marriage is more alive and the love in our family is deeper than ever before," says Liz. "Nothing is routine anymore. Every accomplishment Dustin makes brings new joy. Even the older kids adore their little brother. Dustin wakes up with a smile on his face every morning and spends the day spreading love and happiness."

After Dustin was born, Liz admits she let go of a lot of the control she held in the family. Liz began to turn things over to God and Mike, which helped their marriage and family dynamics. And just watching her husband loving and caring for their three children fills Liz's heart with constant appreciation for the man she married.

"The little things in life don't bother us anymore," explains Mike. "It all melted away after Dustin was born. We realize there is so much we can't control in life, so we accept God's will for us," he says. "I learned there is a reason for everything. There is a good reason Dustin is here. I cannot even imagine how empty our lives would be without him. He has done so many things for us."

Dustin is almost three years old now. His angelic smile and happy babbling captivates everyone around him. Dustin is not just a miracle for the Gary family; he is a miracle for the community. The gifts and cards, including one from their archbishop, still have not stopped coming. People who have followed his story just want to hold and hug Dustin whenever they see him. Some people have told Liz and Mike that Dustin's miracle has changed their lives.

Mike and Liz agree that it was through Dustin that their marriage was reborn. Mike says he is still not big on communicating. Liz admits she is still high-strung, but that she is calmer since Dustin came into their lives. Both now describe themselves as very happily married and in love with each other. Their differences pale next to the bond they now share. The situation that initially seemed like a tragedy turned out to be a blessing for which they thank God every day.

—Patti Maguire Armstrong,
Jeff Cavins, and Matthew Pinto

3

Till Death Do Us Part

"Mommy, where's Daddy?"

Theresa looked down at her innocent little girl, just barely out of diapers. She swallowed hard, smiled, and then told the same lie she always told her children.

"Daddy's still at work, honey. Now let's get you ready for bed so there's time to read a book."

As Theresa called her other four children to start the bedtime routine, she wondered where her husband Paul really was. Of course she knew he was at a bar. *But which one and where? And when will he come home ... or rather* will *he come home this time?* Then, a scary thought pushed its way into her thoughts. *Maybe it would be easier if he never made it home.* But Theresa immediately stopped herself. *No,* she determined, *I won't think like that.* And then Theresa did what she did every night. She prayed. *Please God, bring Paul home safe and please help him to get better.*

Theresa had been praying such a prayer almost since the day they were married in 1976. Besides praying and taking one day at a time, it seemed there was nothing more she could do. She was determined that her children would not come from a broken home. Theresa felt that she had made her choice to marry Paul, and now she had to live with the consequences. All the warning signs had been there from the beginning, but like most young people, Theresa was too naive to recognize them.

By anyone's estimation, Paul and Theresa were the classic odd couple. Quiet, kind, and serious, Theresa was the typical "good girl." She was from a large family, her grades were excellent, she loved school, and she was one of the few kids from her small Western town who did not drink alcohol. Paul, on the other hand, was an only child who hated school, demanded to be the center of attention, had a mean streak a mile long, hated authority, and loved to party.

Theresa's first memory of Paul is crystal clear. She was in third grade and it was her first day at a new school. Paul had bullied her to the point of humiliation. "I hated him," Theresa admits. Ironically, Paul was not a typical bully. Most of the frequent fights he engaged in were to protect the underdog against bigger, more powerful kids. He is not sure why he had picked on Theresa in grade school, but one thing was for sure—as he got older, he definitely wanted her attention.

"She was so pretty," recalls Paul. "By the time I was in junior high, I had a crush on her." Although Paul's eye regularly roved to other girls, he always drifted back to Theresa. He wooed her with gifts; many of them he made himself, such as religious carvings and boxes. Both had come from strong Catholic homes.

Theresa could not help but be flattered by Paul's love notes and gifts. The frequent religious theme of his gifts only endeared him more to her. By their sophomore year of high school, they had begun dating each other exclusively. At times, they broke up and dated others but were eventually drawn back together.

Theresa was active in sports, so she often left town for games and tournaments. Those were the nights Paul indulged in his love for drinking. Theresa strongly disapproved, so he kept away from it until she was away. When she heard of his partying later, she would stew for a day or two. But her disappointment always lifted after Paul's apologies. In reality, Theresa thought that *she* was the odd one since almost everyone she knew drank. She just did not like the taste of alcohol or like to see people get drunk.

After high school graduation, Paul stayed home to work on his parents' farm while Theresa went away to college. Absence made their hearts grow fonder. Without Theresa, Paul felt empty. He feared that some other guy would win her affection. For Theresa, being away from home and her boyfriend left her feeling lost. So they decided to get married.

Theresa's parents expressed concern that she would not be happy in the country feeding chickens. Living in a trailer on Paul's parents' farm was actually fine with Theresa. What bothered her was that, once she married her true love, the romance ended.

"When I had that piece of paper that said she was mine, I did whatever I wanted," says Paul. "I knew she was naive, so I figured I could get away with a lot."

Many nights, Theresa sat outside their trailer and listened to the sounds from town drifting in on the night air. Hidden in the tall grass lest someone stop by, tears poured from her eyes and released the pain. Never had she felt so alone. "I wanted to be with Paul, but not in that environment," Theresa explained. In the beginning she went with him to the bars but it was always the same humiliation. Sitting alone at a table, she would watch Paul circulate through the bar and get drunker. Occasionally, he would stop by the table or send someone over to baby-sit her or ask her to dance. Meanwhile, the liquor would sharpen Paul's mean streak, making him unpleasant to be around.

Without the element of religion in his life, Paul had little conscience and saw no reason not to satisfy his own desires. "I just figured we were two different people," says Paul. "She was a good wife, but I saw her refusal to party as a big flaw."

Theresa clung to the faith of her youth and never missed Mass or stopped praying—especially for Paul. When he was not drinking, Paul was a loving husband. His promises to stop would fill Theresa with hope, but it was always just a matter of time before Paul slipped back into drinking. Still, Theresa kept praying and hoping.

Shortly after their third wedding anniversary, their first child, a son, was born. Theresa was thrilled: "Becoming a mother meant everything to me." Unfortunately, Paul's alcoholism marred this happy occasion. He had quit farming and got a job working on oil rigs across the prairies. Theresa had called Paul at work to let him know she was in labor.

Paul was already drunk when he got the phone call. He had worked midnight to 8 a.m., then went out drinking whiskey in a local bar with friends. By noon, he was drunk. A friend found him in the bar and brought him to the hospital where he promptly passed out.

Theresa's sister was at the hospital. Since Theresa had never said a word to anyone about Paul's drinking, her sister just thought it was "one of those things" and filled him with coffee. Paul's own parents understood their son had a serious problem with alcohol, but they felt helpless to do anything about it. They just kept praying for him. Theresa was too excited about becoming a mother to dwell on another of Paul's drunken bouts.

Fatherhood added a dimension of love which softened Paul. "I wanted my son to have a mom and a dad," he says. "I knew that being a better husband to Theresa would also make me a better father. I knew a person could only take so much, so I checked myself into a treatment program. I did it for Theresa, not for myself."

A year of sobriety brought Theresa great peace. She and Paul discovered how much they both loved parenthood and enjoyed one another's company. It warmed her heart to watch Paul laugh and cuddle with their baby. But one day, while on vacation, Paul had a drink. From that point on, he returned to the vicious cycle of getting drunk, sobering up, apologizing, and then eventually getting drunk again. He did vow to keep alcohol out of the house so he would never drink in front of his family, and this was a vow he kept.

Four more children followed in quick succession. Paul delighted in his family when he was with them. "Daddy's home!" the kids often announced with glee when Paul walked through the door. He played with his children and taught them many things. But Theresa could never count on the good times. She protected her young ones from the truth by telling them Daddy was still at work whenever he failed to come home. There were never any fights or emotional scenes when Paul returned either. Theresa would take Paul aside, away from the children, and quietly plead for him to stop. The tears began to make Paul feel guilty, because he knew he was letting his family down. But rather than stop, Paul drowned his guilt with booze.

While at work, Paul had progressed to almost every kind of drug short of heroin. At the time, drugs flowed freely among oil rig workers. Yes, there was a high rate of accidents and even deaths, but Paul could not keep from indulging. Drugs were actually only an aid to his drinking. Uppers, like crack cocaine and speed, enabled him to go out drinking after work. Then, when he had to turn around and work another shift, the drugs kept him going again.

While Paul continued his dark descent, Theresa began to find self-respect. "As my children grew and I got involved in their lives with coaching and teaching CCD, I realized that Paul was the one with the problem, not me." Theresa derived great pleasure from motherhood. "I felt so alive with my kids. Since my husband preferred drinking to me, I did not feel like a good wife, but I knew I was a good mom." Through teaching and coaching, Theresa discovered she worked well with children in general. Her teams often won tournaments and titles. Once her youngest was in school full-time, Theresa returned to college for a teaching degree.

Theresa's patience with Paul began to grow thin. Often, while delighting in one of the kids' accomplishments, a wave of resentment would wash over her. *Paul has a loving wife and beautiful children, but he's throwing it all away,* she would think. Finally, Theresa told Paul that if he did not sober up by the time their youngest child graduated from high school, she would leave him.

Paul's guilt grew, but then, so did his sin. While Theresa attended college, Paul began a long-term affair with a woman in town. For Paul, this was the first time his adultery was not a case of two drunks going to bed. "I knew Theresa could do better than me, yet I finally realized that I loved her and I did not want to break up our family." Paul confessed, believing that if he told the truth, he would never again be tempted in this way again.

Earlier in their marriage, Theresa realized that Paul's adulterous, one-nights stands were linked to his drinking. This affair was not, though, and it cut through the numbness of her heart to where she could still feel pain.

Haven't I suffered enough? she cried. *Lord, please help us!* Theresa kept praying. There was nothing to do but hold her head high and continue living life as best she could. Theresa was now a sixth-grade teacher and a winning coach. She was determined to continue working hard to be a good mother and wife. By now, however, Theresa was convinced that it was just a matter of time before she left Paul.

Once the kids were in junior high and high school, they began to see their father for what he really was—a drunk. He had been a loving father, and they still loved him. But the relationship had grown cold. Paul also began to challenge Theresa's efforts to raise the children in the Catholic faith. If the kids had stayed out late due to sports, Paul insisted that Theresa not force them to get up and go to church on Sunday. Being teenagers, they usually sided with their dad's argument. Paul did not just deny the existence of God; he often unleashed anger at the mere suggestion that God might exist. Paul was walking and sleeping with the devil, and the devil was working hard to close the deal. At the rate things were going, Paul was easily within his grasp.

The remaining threads of Paul's life began unraveling. A sideline business he had operated for many years completely failed. His kids, now mostly in their teens, no longer looked up to him. He was kicked out of high school coaching, and he had been warned that if there were any more angry outbursts at sporting events, he would be banned from even attending. Often, he wished he was dead, but he did not have the guts to do it himself. There were other times when he was so angry that he could kill those who had offended him. Only the threat of prison stopped him from becoming a murderer.

One summer afternoon, Paul appeared in the center of town ranting and raving at anyone who could hear him. "Something happened to me," Paul remembers. "I was going off the deep end." After shouting threats at the world and bragging about how great he was, Paul got into his car and recklessly sped through town. The police chief, a friend of Paul's, later showed up at his house. Paul sat outside, sobering up away from his family.

"You're in trouble this time," the chief said. "We received twenty-one complaints, Paul. That's a record."

"Did anyone give you a license-plate number?" Paul sneered.

"No," the chief admitted.

"Then you have nothing on me," Paul laughed.

Amazingly, no charges were ever filed. In all his years of drinking and driving, Paul had received warnings but not a single arrest for driving under the influence. The townspeople didn't need a license plate number to prove Paul's guilt. They all knew it was him and they were furious. Some threatened him while others gave him the cold shoulder.

As the "mountain" Paul imagined he was began to crumble, he thought everyone was against him. "It never dawned on me that it was 100 percent my fault," says Paul.

"Then, when I was working on an oil rig in Canada, I was near the end of my rope, physically and mentally. I was deeply depressed. For three days in a row I woke up with fierce hangovers. On the fourth day, I thought to myself: 'I am so, so tired of this life.'"

A born-again Christian at work had been regularly telling Paul to read the Bible. Paul resisted but finally asked what book of the Bible the co-worker would recommend. He suggested the gospel of Matthew. Sitting in his dimly-lit motel room, Paul dug the Gideon's Bible out of a drawer. Once, many years ago, he had tried to read the Bible and found it to be a bunch of mumbo jumbo. Now, holding the Book in his hands, Paul let out a disheartened sigh. He knew that the only one who could help him was God.

Beginning with the birth of Jesus, Paul began reading. Immediately the room's dim light seemed to brighten and illuminate the words. And the words themselves went down with crystal clarity. Paul was spellbound. He felt the love of Jesus and felt His divine presence beside him in that very motel room. Every word seemed to pierce through the cloud of his life and bring light to his being. Through a flood of repentant tears, he read on.

"I understood it all," Paul's says. "That God loved us so much that He sent His only Son, the teachings of Christ, the miracles, the casting out of demons, all the parables, the passion and crucifixion, His resurrection, and His final commissioning of the disciples where He leaves them with the words: 'And behold I am with you always.'"

No drug or drink had ever given Paul the high he experienced through Christ. "Jesus was there with me," he explains. "It was as if He was saying: 'Accept me and I will save you and lead you down the path of love.'"

Paul accepted. The deep, penetrating love of Christ blazed through him. Paul literally began to feel the slime of darkness drain from his being. It did not happen in an instant, but seemed to last around half an hour. As the stink of sin and darkness left, the warmth of love and light began to fill in the spaces. Paul could not feel more ashamed for the sorry state of his soul and yet, as the cleansing love of Jesus washed over him, he never imagined such euphoria.

Jesus had come to Paul and led him by the hand away from evil. "My health was failing, and death would have been around the corner. If I had not accepted Jesus at that moment, I might be in hell right now. Jesus had always been there for me, but I had to be the one to make the decision to turn to Him." In the aftermath, Paul was left with a profound peace that his life would forever be in God's hands. There would be no more drugs or alcohol or women. He would seek to serve God and turn from sin. He spent the day in thanksgiving and prayer. In the morning, Paul awoke refreshed and on fire with love for God.

Paul called Theresa and his mother (who had prayed the Rosary everyday for him for years) to tell them of his experience. He wasn't surprised when both seemed skeptical. After all, there had been so many broken promises. Paul was confident that this time would be different.

When he returned home, one of the first things Paul did was to see a priest and go to confession. He began attending daily Mass and reading the Bible for an hour or two every day. Theresa was in awe. Paul was becoming transformed. When Theresa looked deeply into his eyes now, Paul looked back with love and caring. And when Theresa spoke, she could tell that Paul was really listening to her. The gut wrenching fear for Paul's well-being gave way to trust, love, and joy.

Then, it dawned on Theresa that Paul was outdoing her in the religion department. If her husband was going to start his day with God at Mass, Theresa realized she should be there, too. In spite of all those years of faithful prayers, she had never gone deep enough to fully experience Christ in her life. Now, with the miracle of her husband's conversion, Theresa moved from survival mode to joyfully embracing God's love and power.

"Everything is so different," Theresa explains. "Paul and I are so happy and very much in love. It's like we've been married for four years instead of twenty-nine. We drove to a religious conference recently and the whole time we talked about God and listened to praise music together."

Theresa acknowledges that in today's world, few women would look at her life and think she was blessed. But Theresa says she could not be happier. "I'm happy I married Paul," she says. "Those were hard years, but none of it was wasted. I would do it again."

One of the greatest joys that keeping her marriage vows brings Theresa is the knowledge that her family stayed together. She and Paul both admit that healing is necessary when a family has been through the turmoil they experienced, but they are deeply grateful that they rode it out. Together, they can now experience the peace and love of healing. The children, some married with their own children, see the dramatic difference in their father accomplished by God's saving power. Paul has told his children that he is sorry for all the hurt he caused them, and he is working on building a new relationship with them.

"I'm so grateful for my kids and that our family made it," he says. "We stayed together and everyone is glad. It's a whole new family. We sit around and love each other and visit all night long. Instead of just stopping the hurt, the wound healed."

On the day of his conversion, Paul knew that there would be hard work ahead but he knew there was no turning back. Through the priest that serves as both his and Theresa's spiritual director, he came to realize that the devil was going to fight his conversion. Paul was tempted to feel angry and critical toward those that hurt him. In the beginning he wrestled with the devil for days, thinking his prayers were not working and that he could never really maintain his new life. His spiritual director encouraged him by explaining that it was part of the process of his continual conversion. The harder Paul fought back with prayer, Eucharistic adoration, and Mass, the stronger he became. "It took patience, and my spiritual director helped me a lot," says Paul. "In the end, the devil is a coward who runs in the face of God. The Lord is my defense."

Paul realizes that he, too, was once a coward, putting up a tough exterior but lacking true inner strength. He cannot find the words to express appreciation for Theresa's undying commitment and prayers. "Our love grows every day," Paul explains. "It is so amazing. I did not know real love until I knew the love of God. Once you experience that, it's unbelievable."

—Patti Maguire Armstrong,
Jeff Cavins, and Matthew Pinto

4
The Second Time Around

Tossing and turning on the small couch in her living room, anger and bitterness chased away any chance for sleep from Irene McWilliams. "How did I get into this mess?" she cried. "I should have known better than to get married again. Being alone was better than this nightmare."

Meanwhile, Rick lay awake in bed. *I've lost her,* he thought sadly. *I keep trying to make everyone happy, but it seems that no one is happy.*

It was the second marriage for both of them; both had been rejected by unfaithful spouses who had looked for love outside their marriages. Rick and Irene never again wanted to experience the searing pain of rejection, and they thought they had entered this marriage cautiously. But in reality, they had sought comfort and security. They had rushed into their relationship before the ink had barely dried on Rick's divorce papers.

Rick had been raising his three daughters since his wife had left town with another man. Rick did not let her go without a fight; he went after her to bring her home. But she was restless. Marriage and motherhood were not enough for her. "Our marriage is over," she told him.

So Rick's divorce was not even final when he met Irene in a bar one evening in 1991. Irene was familiar with Rick's story; she had lived it herself six years earlier. Her husband had left her for another woman. Her ex-husband fought hard to keep their two children from Irene and turned every visitation into a tug-of-war. It was particularly hard on their daughter who had always been a "daddy's girl." Their son was closer to Irene. Eventually, Irene gained full custody of her son, while her ex-husband got custody of their daughter. It was a painful ripping apart of their family.

Irene knew the degradation of being tossed aside like a dirty old sock. She listened to Rick's pain and shared her own. It was such a comfort for Rick to have someone to talk to, someone who understood and seemed to care. Rick took Irene home and they talked until the sun came up.

"Well, if you ever need to talk to anyone, give me a call," Irene told Rick hopefully.

Rick went home, tired from lack of sleep and confused by his feelings. The pain of his failed marriage was still raw. The last thing he was looking for was another woman in his life. Yet there had been a spark. Irene was interested in him; that much was obvious. He had not experienced that sort of attention for a very long time.

Although Irene was on his mind, Rick avoided calling her at first. *What am I thinking?* he would scold himself until the urge to call had passed. But the urge kept returning until eventually Rick called her two weeks after their first meeting.

"Hello, is this Irene?" the male voice asked after Irene answered the phone. Her heart skipped a beat. Even though she had been attracted to Rick, she knew it was foolish to expect anything.

His wife might not even go through with the divorce, she thought. But when she heard Rick's voice again, she could not restrain her hopes. Irene knew from their late-night conversation that Rick was kind and loving. And he was loyal, something Irene had not experienced in the men in her life.

They went out and conversation again came easily. Rick's wife followed through on her plan to end their marriage. By the time the divorce became final, Rick admitted to himself that he was falling in love with Irene. The female attention felt good. Irene was comforting, caring, and loving. Rick tried to be cautious and rational. He continued attending Mass every Sunday and regularly asked God to lead the way. *If this is not meant to be, then nothing will come of it,* he determined.

Irene had only recently returned to attending her Protestant church, and this was only at her son's prodding. She had been angry at God for all the pain and abandonment she had suffered. *Why wasn't God there to fix everything?* she had wondered.

As Irene and Rick's relationship progressed, Rick invited Irene to attend Saturday evening Mass with him and his girls. He was pleasantly surprised by her ready agreement. Irene and her son came to enjoy the services with Rick.

Although they had known each other only since October, they were soon planning to be married in July, less than a year after they had met. *We are older and wiser,* Irene thought as she embarked on a second marriage. *Rick is different, he would never leave me.*

But their kids were not swept up with the same enthusiasm for a new, blended family life. All of them—Rick's girls and Irene's son—still hurt from the brokenness of having one of their parents leave. No one was excited about the prospect of a "replacement parent."

During their honeymoon in Hawaii, Rick and Irene were euphoric in their love for each other and the promise of happiness for the future. They were confident that their love would carry them through the adjustment of making their new family work. Irene and her son would soon move in with Rick and his daughters. They discussed the expected trials that lay ahead such as step-parenting, visitations, and the teen years that three of the four kids were in. Everything seemed manageable on the wings of love.

Irene and Rick had barely returned home when the honeymoon came to a screeching halt. Rick's sister, who had been taking care of the kids, filled them in on what had transpired while they were away. Rick's ex-wife had showed up unexpectedly demanding the girls. His sister refused to let them go, fearing the mom would disappear with them. The police were called in. Examining the divorce settlement, an officer decreed that the mom had the right to take the girls for the day. When it was an hour-and-a-half past the agreed upon return time, Rick's sister went looking for them. She found them in a shopping mall, and again the police had to be called in.

All the strength and confidence Irene had once felt about becoming Rick's wife and stepmother to his daughters began to evaporate. The girls let Irene know that they resented her presence. "You aren't our mom!" they often screamed at her.

"I'm not trying to take your mom's place," Irene would patiently explain. "I'm just trying to help take care of you." Irene's son was cordial to Rick but there was a great distance between them. He went from having his mother to himself to having to share her with Rick and the three girls. It was not an arrangement he wanted.

To make matters worse, Rick's ex-wife encouraged her daughters to be as bad as they could in order to get rid of Irene. The girls took the challenge seriously and did everything in their power to make Irene miserable.

Rick worked a swing shift. This meant that half the time he was home, but the other half Irene was left to run the household alone. She worked from 5 a.m. until 1 p.m. so she was home when the kids returned from school. "I'm just an abused baby-sitter," Irene began to think. She tried to bring rules and structure into the household but the girls hated her for it. They were used to an easy-going dad who did not make a big deal if they pushed the limits. As far as they were concerned, Irene was the Wicked Witch of the West.

Rick had always been a peacemaker. He hated conflict, so he avoided it. He thought if he just loved everyone enough, somehow it would all work out. But it became clear that everyone was vying against each other for his attention. Rick responded by trying to spend every moment at home giving to his family, but not as a unit because they resented each other so deeply. During the day he would give his all to the girls and try to have some sort of relationship with his stepson. After the kids went to bed, Rick considered his time with Irene to be sacred. But his plan was not working. Things kept getting worse.

Then, Irene's aunt Gladys came to live with them. She was elderly and needed help. Rick naturally wanted to help someone in need, especially a relative of his wife's. He tried to be more and more loving, but the plan again failed. Aunt Gladys attempted to be the replacement mother that the girls had already made clear they did not want. Relationships were strained until the household often exploded with tension and anger. Aunt Gladys soon realized it would be best if she moved to a senior care facility. This brought some relief, but the family remained in crisis.

"Maybe it will help if I became Catholic," thought Irene. "Then Rick and I will really be one." They investigated what it would take and learned that both of them needed to have their first marriages annulled. In the eyes of the Church, they were still married to their first spouses. Unless the Church determined that their first marriages were not valid—performed without full understanding and commitment—they could not be married in the Catholic Church.

After they went through the process and both were granted annulments, Irene took official catechism instruction. In 1995, three years into the marriage, she was received into the Catholic Church. Both Rick and Irene had high hopes that this would be the beginning of the end of their struggles, but it wasn't. Nothing got better.

Seeking help and guidance, Irene and Rick met with a priest a couple of times. He offered them comfort and prayers, but had no solutions to their problems.

Again, Irene shut God out of her life. *Where is God when I need Him?* she wondered angrily. *I'm praying and going to Church. I even became Catholic,* she thought, *but nothing seems to matter. If things are this bad when I'm trying to follow God, then maybe it's time to give up,* she concluded. Irene was not just giving up on God, but on Rick also. "It's over," she told him. "This whole marriage was a huge mistake."

Rick was devastated. He felt like he was trying to bail out the Titanic with a spoon. But still, he was not willing to surrender. *Dear God,* he often prayed, *please help us. I don't know what we need, but you do. Please, at least give us some hope. Show us that there will be a rainbow somewhere at the end of this storm.*

Then, one Sunday, Rick noticed an announcement in the church bulletin. "Troubled Marriage? Retrouvaille can help." he read. When he showed it to Irene she was unimpressed.

"We have to at least try this," Rick pleaded.

"OK, sure. Go ahead and make the arrangements and I'll show up," she reluctantly agreed. *I'll go along with this and then I'm out of here,* Irene thought to herself. In her mind, her marriage to Rick was already a sunken ship. She was not looking for a lifeboat; she wanted a new life.

Rick made the arrangements and the two showed up on Friday for a sort of weekend retreat. There were a number of other couples present. All the meetings were group sessions. Everyone remained anonymous and no one was pressured to speak up but could if they chose to. The leaders shared their own marriage recovery stories. Then, the group was taught a series of listening skills. Everyone was led through an exercise in self-discovery in order to dig deep and see themselves the way others saw them.

For Irene and Rick it was more than eye-opening—it was *heart-opening*.

Rick realized that, at home, he was putting his head in the sand and making Irene play the role of bad guy with the kids. On the surface, Rick looked like the good guy—the one who loved everyone and wanted everyone to be happy. But Rick took a deeper look and realized that he played this role at Irene's expense. Rick wanted to love everyone and have everyone love him. He was not willing to do any disciplining and risk his children's anger. He left that completely to Irene. She had to make and enforce the rules. Rick dodged all the bullets and instead put his wife on the firing line without reinforcements.

Rick realized their marriage and family required him to be stronger. He needed to make the difficult decisions and stop dumping it all on Irene. It was a painful realization because Rick was perfectly comfortable with his head in the sand. But the fear of losing Irene was more than he wanted to bear. He lifted his head high and apologized to Irene for being so selfish.

When Irene looked into herself, she found bitterness and anger. Her heart had grown cold and mean. She was not the person she wanted to be. It was not the sort of wife she had envisioned becoming. Touched by the realization that, in spite of it all, Rick still loved her, Irene's heart grew warm again. Once she let Rick's love back in, Irene realized that she needed to let God back into her life too. Here, she had been pushing out the love of both God and her husband. No wonder her life was out of control.

Three years earlier, Irene and Rick had celebrated the union of their love during their Hawaiian honeymoon. Now they realized that their "love" at that time was merely infatuation. The three years of hell they had been through ultimately became the fire that tested the strength of their love. Without God, they are convinced they would have lost the fight. But by turning to God and each other, a deeper love began to grow—something with roots.

When Irene and Rick returned home Sunday evening, the kids immediately noticed a difference. There was a gentle strength between them. Rick began taking control of the family and followed through with consequences when they tested his newfound authority. And test they did. *This won't last,* they thought of the new Dad. They waited for the old Dad to return but he never did. In the long run, no one missed him. Little by little, the turmoil lessened and peace grew. It was not overnight, but Rick and Irene were in it for the long haul now. With Rick's love and his new support, Irene took less of the flak. This reduced the tension in her own life and made things much better. And once she felt God and Rick's love, Irene was able to show more love rather than anger at everyone.

Last year, eight years after Rick and Irene recommitted themselves to each other, Irene suffered a stroke when a golf-ball sized aneurysm broke in her brain. There was no warning. She and Rick had just enjoyed a pleasant afternoon shopping together. After they returned home, Irene suddenly went numb and called out for Rick. He put her in bed and called 911. At the hospital they learned that most people die on the spot when an aneurysm in the brain breaks open.

The girls, now grown and living away from home, rushed to the hospital to be with Irene. After years of doing their best to get rid of her, no one wanted to lose her. "We did not see it then, but we now realize how much you cared and how much you did for us," one of the girls said. "We are sorry for all the things we did to you," said another. "I can't believe you stayed with dad after all the hell we put you through."

Rick has left his job to care for Irene around the clock. He assists with her physical therapy which has helped her regain much of her abilities. Irene still suffers some slight paralysis and uses a wheelchair.

Irene says she shudders to think of what her life would be like had she followed through on her plan to leave Rick. He is really everything she had hoped to find during her many years alone. Irene says she was blind to this for a time until God opened her eyes.

Together, they survive financially on Irene's disability payments. "We don't need much," Rick explains. "As long as we have each other, that's the most important thing." He adds: "Twice, I almost lost her. Once through divorce and once when she almost left this earth. I am so grateful to God that we are still together."

—Patti Maguire Armstrong,
Jeff Cavins, and Matthew Pinto

5

Looking For Love

Newly married, Tim and I clasped hands as we walked down the church aisle. Our wide smiles reflected the joy and excitement we felt as we began our new life. We knew, of course, that like any married couple we would face challenges and trials. But on that happy day we never could have anticipated that we would have to overcome an obstacle that most people would consider insurmountable. This trial would test our ability to trust each other and challenge our belief in God. It would even drive Tim to consider ending his life.

Such a notion was inconceivable to me when we were dating. From the first time I met Tim I loved his gentle, easy-going style, and how he made me laugh so much. He tells me that he loved how confident and friendly I could be. We loved going to rock concerts and Philadelphia Flyers hockey games, watching movies like *West Side Story* and *Field of Dreams*. We'd go to relative's Baptisms and First Communions. We'd attend Saturday night Mass together and then go to dinner. One of our favorite hang-outs was a neighborhood pub where we'd laugh and eat things we shouldn't—fries, wings, beer. We had a lot of mutual friends.

One Saturday night Tim drove us to our favorite restaurant, but before we got out of the car, he began fumbling in his coat pocket. He seemed nervous, and I was baffled, until he pulled out a ring and asked me to marry him. I was totally surprised but immediately said "Yes!"

I loved the simple way he proposed. Tim says he should have done it with more fireworks and pizzazz, but it was special to me. I loved Tim so much and I knew that we could have a good marriage. He says that he felt God calling him to be with me from the very first day he met me.

During our dating days, there was time for romance and we were really attracted to each other. It was hard to be chaste. But we waited until we were married for two reasons. First, Tim and I believed the Catholic Church's teaching that premarital sex was sinful. Second, one of my sisters had gotten pregnant as a teenager, and it devastated my parents. I was afraid of getting pregnant and putting my parents through that pain all over again. Tim understood and supported me, and I respected him even more for not pressuring me into premarital sex. We both feel proud that we waited to fully give ourselves to one another on our wedding night.

Those first few years of marriage were good. We both enjoyed being married and relished being parents when our two beautiful little girls were born. I was working part-time as a teacher while Tim worked full-time as a factory manager. But we had a few unexpected financial difficulties, and it seemed like it would be better for us if I returned to work full-time. I think it was hard on Tim's pride. He thought he should be able to provide more for his family. He decided that he should work a later shift at the factory so that he could earn more money. He didn't talk to me about this decision. He just made the switch and told me about it afterwards. This meant that he worked all night, then walked through the door at 7 a.m. to help the kids get ready for school as I was leaving for work. He did errands, cleaned a little and made something for dinner, then went to sleep for five hours before heading back to work. I put in a full day at the school and then came home to dinner with the kids. I was alone every night helping them with homework, bathing them, and putting them to bed. It was exhausting.

We were both working a lot of hours and had no time together during the week. Weekends were devoted to the kids' activities. We didn't have much time or energy for our marriage. I resented his work schedule and his complaining about the work he had to do around the house. He seemed to resent having to help out when I was at work. Communication became superficial. We forgot the dreams we shared. We stopped planning for the future. Faith was not a big part of our daily lives. We tried to go to church on Sundays, but we never prayed together. We went through the motions with God, the same way we were going through the motions with each other.

We no longer enjoyed our previously satisfying sex life. We both became self-centered. We were creatures of habit, taking each other for granted, with one day running into the next. I wouldn't acknowledge how desolate our marriage had become. I told myself that as isolated as we had grown, our marriage was still better than my parents' distant marriage had been. And our marriage was better than the cold relationship of Tim's parents, one in which his mother and depressed father rarely interacted. So we convinced ourselves that things between us weren't all that awful. It wasn't great, but we could live with it. What more could we expect? After all, the honeymoon doesn't last forever.

About this time, a new teacher was hired at the school where I worked. Warm, flattering, and encouraging, my new colleague showed a lot of interest in my life. We started spending a lot of time together and I began sharing more of my thoughts and feelings than I had the time or inclination to share with Tim. Suddenly someone was telling me that I was special, smart, and talented. Who wouldn't be flattered? I started making excuses for why I had to work late. I even brought my friend home after work to spend time with my kids while Tim was away. This wasn't shocking or suspicious for one simple reason: My new friend was a woman.

Tim thought it was good for me to have someone to hang out with on weeknights when he was not available. He saw that I seemed happier having my friend Karen around. He would never have encouraged our friendship if he had known that Karen was telling me she loved me and wanted to be with me. Karen had had many sexual encounters with women, and while I was mildly curious about what it would be like to be intimate with a woman, I had never crossed that line. When Karen came on to me, I was at a low point in my life. I was feeling lonely in my marriage, overwhelmed with my responsibilities, and unappreciated. Here was this new person filling the void between Tim and me. She told me I was wonderful. She told me she admired me. And she told me I was beautiful inside and out.

The night I definitely crossed the line with Karen, I knew it was wrong. I knew I had marital vows. I knew I had children. But the temptation to be with Karen was so strong. I felt so alive when I was around her. I felt that jolt of being in love that I used to feel with Tim. I had a diversion from my mid-life drudgery. I knew that I should have flown from the temptation after that night when we crossed the line, but instead I continued the relationship. Karen had gotten herself into my head, and I couldn't imagine life without her. I began comparing this lover to my spouse. Weighed against my years of resentments and the distance between me and Tim, the relationship with Karen seemed too good to give up. Once I had succumbed to the temptation, it was even harder to resist. I didn't want to give up the new excitement I had found—even if it was killing me with guilt—to try to get closer to Tim, especially because it seemed as if he and I were moving further apart each day.

Karen told me she didn't want to come between me and my kids. She said she didn't want to be the cause of my marriage breaking up. She didn't want to put me in a position to have to choose. She sounded so concerned for my well-being and so selfless as she encouraged me to hang on to my relationship with my kids and not leave my husband because of her. But in the next breath, she would tell me how much she wanted to be with me, how much she missed me, how wonderful it would be if we could be together all the time. She was engaging me emotionally and sexually in such a deep bonding way that I had less desire to try to make things work with my husband, who had no idea that I was even cheating on him. Once I slid down that slippery path, it was harder than ever to think about making my marriage whole again.

I can see now that much of my marital discontent came from the distance Tim and I had allowed in our marriage and from some unresolved family-of-origin issues. But Karen told me that I had been unhappy in my marriage because I was truly gay and had simply denied it. The magazines, newspapers, and television shows I watched certainly suggested that anyone who had any homosexual feelings would be unhappy trying to live a heterosexual lifestyle. I began questioning the way I had lived my life for years. At that time it was so easy to blame any unhappiness in my life on the seductive thought that I had chosen the wrong spouse. I began wondering if I would have been much happier if I had pursued the gay lifestyle instead of the traditional male-female relationship.

This was not the first time that I'd ever had a sexual attraction to a woman. I had struggled with an attraction to one of my best friends in high school. We even kissed once. But at that time, it was less socially acceptable to live a gay lifestyle. There were no public school education programs that praised and encouraged homosexuality as an "alternate lifestyle." Though my friend was also attracted to me, she was deathly afraid of anyone finding out. I was just as afraid of rejection by others. We just went on like good friends and never talked about it again.

I am the youngest of five children, four girls and one boy. As a child, I hungered for the affection and attention of my parents, but both were in short supply. I saw that my father paid a lot of attention to my brother, John. For twelve years I did my best to be John's shadow, doing whatever he did because my father would give me some of his attention. When dad was around, he was peaceful and affectionate. He would pray the Rosary daily and he modeled more faith and belief in God than mom did. This made an impact on me. I loved my father's warm smile and gentleness, so I became a tomboy to get his attention. Dad was more interested in John's successes than mine, but I competed as much as I could in sports with my brother. This was a way I could spend time with my father.

My mother had little time for me or my older sisters. I wanted her love and attention, but she didn't seem to be able to be loving and gentle with her kids. She yelled a lot. Looking back, I can say that I think she was probably depressed and overwhelmed with five children and no help from my father. My father worked the third shift during the week. My mom was frustrated and stressed out. Dad worked all night and wasn't available to help mom in the evenings. She became physically and verbally abusive. She was like a punitive drill sergeant who yelled all the time. It would make me want to hide under my bed. You knew not to ask any questions and just do what you were told. She seemed to care more about the house and how it looked than interacting with her kids. I don't remember her ever telling me that she loved me.

When I was twelve, John's friends were beginning to notice the differences between boys and girls. They decided they didn't want to play with a girl anymore. They shunned me. I was totally cut off from the life I had known. It was further devastating to lose some of the attention I had gained from my father. I had no place to belong anymore, and I felt lonely and left out. I was socialized to fit in with my brother and his interests and didn't know how to do the feminine things the other girls my age were interested in.

I asked my mother for help and tried to spend more time with her, but she ignored me. She was concerned only with my getting the chores done, frequently berating me about my school work instead of helping me with something I didn't understand. She didn't role-model any feminine interests for me at all. I loved my mother then and I love her now, but she just didn't have the capacity to give me what I needed.

So I started to associate with other girls who were athletic and jocks, and I adapted over time. I learned to feel more comfortable around women, but it felt like I was missing some key knowledge or experience about what it meant to be feminine. I desperately wanted to fit in and belong with the other girls my age, but it was difficult because I had spent so much time trying to identify with my brother, to think and act in a way that would help me fit in with him and his friends. I think it made me more confident and assertive. But it came at the expense of my developing normally with my female peers.

I was able to push any thoughts about same-sex attraction out of my head because I was motivated to do so. In the 1960s and '70s, homosexuality was not considered an option, so I didn't waste my time cultivating an appetite for something that was not possible in my world. I had some attraction to boys throughout my teen years, so I just focused my attention on dating boys. Plus I knew that I wanted to have children and raise them in a stable home. I thought I had enough attraction towards men that I could pursue a normal married life. I directed my thoughts towards trying to connect in an appropriate way with the men and women in my life.

When I met Tim, he reminded me of some of my father's best qualities. I was attracted to him and wanted to be with him for the rest of my life. But I didn't know that those same-sex attraction feelings I'd had when I was younger would come back so strongly when I was in my forties. Karen definitely pursued me, and the attention was flattering. She knew that I was lonely in my marriage and she stepped right in the middle of that space that Tim and I had allowed to grow between us. I never thought that I would be the type to have an affair. I always valued honesty and integrity. And here I was sneaking around. Lying. Cheating. Giving my heart, mind, body, and soul to someone who knew all the right words to say to flatter me and draw me in. The affair with Karen isolated me from Tim. It strangled my affection for him like a poisonous vine.

When I got caught up in the emotions of the affair it felt like the "falling in love" kind of feelings that I used to have with Tim. I see now that some of the dissatisfaction I felt in my marriage was a natural effect of not spending any time with Tim and my holding on to old resentments. But I started to tell myself that my dissatisfaction with my marriage was due to my feelings of same-sex attraction. It was my catch-all excuse for any unhappiness in my life at that time. If I was unhappy, I could blame it on something the media told me I had no control over. If I was unhappy, I could find a thousand therapists to tell me that I could only find happiness by embracing the gay lifestyle. If I was unhappy, the culture told me sexual fulfillment would make me happy. I told myself I had a right to be happy. I thought that my lover would complete my happiness.

Tim knew something wasn't right, but he couldn't put his finger on it. He had tried to be more available and attentive, but I was unreceptive. I was torn. It was like being a train on a track that suddenly splits down the middle in two directions. I was being pulled by Karen on the left and Tim on the right. But I was leaning towards Karen. I was telling Tim I was unhappy. In my mind I was identifying myself as a lesbian. I had cut my hair short and spiky. I had even adapted more assertive mannerisms and masculine clothes. I began hanging out with other lesbians and enjoying the camaraderie that I had always longed for. It finally came to the point that I decided to leave my husband.

I'll never forget the night I told Tim I wanted to leave. I was afraid that he would get mad and yell and scream. But he was stunned. He just sat down and wept. He wondered if he had done something to make me want to be gay. He begged me for another chance. I yelled back that I was born with same-sex attraction and couldn't change, and that I'd been unhappy for some time. I said that I was sorry to hurt him like this, but it wasn't meant to be. I was gay, after all, and there was nothing I could do about it.

Within a few days of my telling Tim, he became depressed and suicidal. He said he didn't want to live anymore. I had never seen him so devastated. I was so sad to be the cause of so much pain to him. I thought about the good years we had enjoyed together. I thought about our two girls, how I had promised to be with him for the rest of our lives. I thought about how my decision to leave would take him away from our daughters, force us to sell the house, and leave him alone. I realized I couldn't leave him while he was so depressed. He needed to see a counselor and he wanted me to come with him. It was the least I could do for him.

Seeing Tim's pain caused me to rethink my decision to leave. I realized the depth of my compassion and care for him. I did not want to hurt this man. I did not know if I would be able to be happy with him again, but I knew he deserved for me to try. He at least deserved my making the effort to find out where our relationship got off track and how my same-sex attraction feelings had gotten out of control. I turned to my father for advice.

My dad told me, "Sarah, God's given you a beautiful family. Think about what you're doing and feeling. Pray about it … stay with the church. Get help from a good therapist. If you need money for counseling, I'll pay for it. People can be attracted to any being—either the same sex or the opposite sex. But it's what you do about it and how you behave and act on it. That's what matters."

His advice helped me. I went to confession, where my parish priest referred me to a therapist who works with people with my problem. I discussed with the counselor some of the key factors that can spur the development of homosexuality: distant relationship with parent of the same sex, peer rejection, weak masculine or feminine identity, poor body image, and sexual abuse. My history showed several of those factors.

I worked on forgiving my mother for her harsh treatment and neglect of me. I turned to the Blessed Virgin Mary as another loving mother who could care for me in ways that my earthly mother wasn't able to. I worked on identifying with more of my feminine qualities by asking God to help me appreciate my feminine beauty. I turned to God as my loving Father who could unconditionally love and accept me and be crazy about me whether I am hitting a home run in baseball or knitting a pink sweater. And I tried to be careful about whether I indulged in thoughts that would help my marriage heal or would encourage me to harm my marriage. It was not easy. Though I saw progress in the reduction of same-sex attraction thoughts, I still had difficulty letting go. God can give us the tools to help us heal, but we have to *want* the healing. He gave me the tools I needed, but I did not want to fully give myself over to His plan for my life. Despite Tim's objections, I insisted on keeping Karen in my life as a friend. I stopped going to counseling after a couple of months.

Tim started seeing a counselor to help him with his depression and low self-confidence. He became so depressed that he started taking medication. He started working on his self-defeating pattern of thinking and his anxiety. He was working harder on himself than I was working on myself. We were making progress as a couple, but I was like an alcoholic who thought I could stay sober and still hang out in a bar. Karen kept coming on to me. After several months, I found myself telling Tim I wanted to leave. It is so true that if you are not making progress you are sliding backwards. The Bible says that if God helps you clean your house, you had better keep it clean after that or the devil will bring back more temptations when he returns—and I had not kept my house or my mind clean from the temptation.

This time, Tim would not stand for it. He had grown in his self-respect and assertiveness. He knew he didn't deserve to be treated like a doormat. He said he needed to leave for a few days to think things over. He was angry and his heart was hardening towards me to the point that he wanted nothing to do with me. I saw how I was devastating him by my wavering. I also got a taste of what life would be like as a single parent when I had the kids for four days by myself. I knew that whatever Karen could offer me, it wasn't worth the kind of pain it was causing my husband, my kids, and myself. Around the time Tim left, I was at a school picnic and I saw all these happy families together laughing. Carefree kids were running around on a beautiful spring night, and it killed me to think I might have thrown that all away. This time I was the one begging and pleading with Tim to give me one last chance to make things better. He told me I needed to cut all ties with Karen and go back to counseling before he would consider coming home.

I had not seen my therapist in months, but I called her crying and saying that I needed help. I asked her if it was too late to save my marriage. What she said terrified me. "Ask God for a miracle," she told me. I didn't think miracles were for ordinary people like me. And don't you have to be in a hopeless situation to need something like a miracle to make it better? How had I let things get to the point that I needed a miracle?

It was during this time, when Tim was at Mass with me and the kids, that he decided to try to make our marriage strong again. He saw his family around him in God's house and he thought that he really didn't want to be anywhere else, even if the process was going to be painful. He just started sobbing. He saw that the pain was not going to be unending, pointless suffering, but rather a healing pain—like how a doctor must sometimes break a bone that has set poorly and then reset the bones so the person's leg can heal properly.

Tim had the courage to risk trusting that God could heal our marriage and heal me.

Tim saw me making amends to him and working on myself with twice the diligence that he had hoped for when I first told him about the affair. I knew things were bad, but when I realized that I had hit rock bottom, I became ready to do whatever needed to be done to save my marriage. I told Karen I couldn't see her anymore. I prayed in front of the Blessed Sacrament nearly every day. I was open to the counselor's suggestions, and I faithfully followed through with the work I needed to do on myself. I held nothing back this time. I asked God to help me to know how much he loved me and forgave me. I asked God every day to give me strength and to make me the best wife and mother and worker that I could possibly be for that day. Any time a same-sex attraction thought came into my head, I quickly focused on a different thought that would support my marriage. Same-sex attraction was not an option for me, and I couldn't afford to harbor any thoughts about it for even a second. I used some principles from the twelve-step programs to help me get beyond my temptations.

I committed myself to appreciating my God-given feminine qualities. The softening of my heart towards my mother and myself coincided with the softening of my hard, outward appearance. I learned to trust that God had a beautiful plan for my life and that being born a woman was a blessing rather than a curse. I did not have to be ashamed to be a woman. I was relieved that I did not have to hide my soft side with assertive bravado. Tim was becoming a strong, assertive man whom I could lean upon to support me. I found myself even more attracted to him than I had been even during the honeymoon days of our marriage. Our sex life revived with such beautiful passion and gratitude.

Today, we take nothing for granted. We see every day as a gift. Every time I have his hand to hold it is a miracle.

I praise my husband for not just blaming me and walking away from me for my mistakes and my woundedness. He upheld his marital vow "in sickness and in health." He gave me the time I needed to heal and he was humble enough to look at the distance that we had both allowed to grow between us. He took ownership for not being present to me. I asked his forgiveness for pulling away from him and for the affair, for holding on to resentments, for not fleeing from temptation.

It is such a relief to say "yes" to God's will for me instead of fighting against it. God has given me a full and complete healing. It astounds me how one can be in the darkest of dark places and think there is nothing to live for. And then to see how God steps in, offering hope and healing.

I was very fortunate to have my husband persevere with me. It has been two years since the affair, and we thank God every day for giving us the grace to keep us on His path and in line with His plan for our lives.

Forgiveness is essential if one is to truly be healed—forgiveness by God, by one's spouse, and oneself. With God's grace, any trial can be overcome.

—as told to Christine Wittman

Christine Wittman *is a licensed therapist and free-lance writer. She works as an individual and marital counselor and is a conference speaker in the Archdioceses of Philadelphia and Washington. She and her husband, Mark, have been married for eight years and are presenters for Marriage Encounter and Engaged Encounter. She can be reached at christinewittman@comcast.net.*

Information about approaches to the prevention and healing of same-sex attraction can be obtained in the Catholic Medical Association's research paper, "Homosexuality and Hope," listed on their website www.cathmed.org.

6

Paradise: Lost and Found

As my husband, Sam, drove off in anger, I imagined how I would feel if he got into an accident and died. Would I care? The answer frightened me. Such a scenario would accomplish what I did not have the guts to do—end our miserable marriage. Hating my own husband felt like acid eating away at my insides. It was not my desire. I wanted to provide a happy, peaceful home for our four sons, but I felt that Sam made it impossible.

I had promised myself that I would never get stuck in such a miserable marriage. I was smart and did not have to settle for anything less than the perfect mate. During college, a friend and I often analyzed the bad marriages we witnessed among relatives. We wondered how it happened that couples who once loved each other had become angry or indifferent. Where had the love gone?

My friend and I were idealistic. We had plenty of men to choose from and were determined to select our spouses wisely. When I fell in love, however, I did not actually know how to choose wisely. My parameters boiled down to someone who was smart, ambitious, and who loved me and treated me well.

There had been many suitors over the years, but there was always a missing spark. Sam was different. Or maybe it was the conditions under which we met that were different. After getting a masters degree in business administration, I took a contract job for an American company in the South

Pacific. I wanted something exotic, and I found it in a tropical paradise. Learning a new language and working amidst palm trees, beaches, and balmy weather satisfied my craving for adventure. Almost from the moment I stepped off the plane, I had suitors lined up. Not a one interested me, however, until Sam.

We met at the airport. He was a media specialist in charge of setting up communication networks throughout the area. Sam had just returned from a six-week business trip in California and was surprised to see a new face on the island. I was at the airport to pick up some packages. We waited for the luggage to unload together.

I knew immediately that Sam was interested, and I accepted his invitation for lunch in the airport lounge. Over lunch, I determined that Sam was not only friendly, but also intelligent and interesting. During the next few weeks, we continued to get together casually. At first, I tried to keep my distance. Years of boyfriends who became too serious while I lost interest made me cautious.

In fact, before I left the United States, I asked God to find the right man for me. Contemplating my past romances, it occurred to me that my weak attempts at practicing my Catholic faith had always met with resistance from those I dated. I asked God to find the person He wanted me to marry, and that he be someone who helped me to do a better job at practicing my faith. I discovered later that Sam had also prayed for God to find the right spouse for him. Sam was Catholic, although he was as bad at practicing his faith as I was. In general, neither one of us made religion a top priority.

After a few weeks of courtship, our feelings for one another grew strong. I considered the possibility that he might be "the one." When Sam left for another two-week business trip, the love letters I received from him were the icing on top of the cake. By the time he returned we were "in love."

Our now-passionate romance made us almost inseparable. We planned a wedding a year from the date we met in the airport. My family was enthusiastic, trusting that I knew what I was doing. Sam's family was cool to the idea, thinking this fast romance would blow over. At the end of six months, Sam's employment contract was up. I quit my job so we could move together to the West Coast. Rather than setting up separate housekeeping for the six months before our wedding, we moved in together. Both our parents were unhappy with the arrangement. Since they were of an older generation, it neither surprised nor concerned us. We were going to be married soon anyway, so we failed to see why it bothered them.

Unfortunately, our parents did not really hand much religion down to us. Perhaps if we had known better the teachings of the Bible and the Church we might have had a clue that it was not just our parents who were unhappy with the arrangement but God, too. If we knew that "the two shall become one flesh," referred to God's teaching that sexual union was a gift for those who had become one in marriage, we might have considered waiting until we were married. Had we been concerned with the Church's teachings, we would have understood the sacredness of marriage as opposed to just "playing house." With a little enlightenment, we would have desired to follow God's teachings in order to benefit from His protection. Instead, we went on our merry, ignorant way. Neither one of us had ever cared about what we saw as the intricacies of our faith. Since we were adults, I don't blame our parents. But our lack of a solid religious foundation definitely made it easier to live together.

The marriage preparation required by the Catholic Church at that time did little to help us. Along with a dozen or so other engaged couples, we listened to a six-week series of speakers. They—and their marriages—seemed way too dull. Since we considered our relationship to be incredibly romantic and exciting, we could not relate to the middle-aged (and older) couples who gave advice on how to have a happy marriage. So what if they had been married thirty or forty years? Sam and I had no intention of traveling down their dull path.

Early one July morning, before the sun was up, Sam and I hopped into our white sports car and headed east. Our wedding had been planned long-distance, since we were to be married in Wisconsin in the church in which I had been baptized. Just weeks before we left for the wedding, however, Sam and I began to have some serious arguments. At times, I found him to be completely irrational. He stubbornly refused to discuss many issues. He was, however, apologetic and romantic after we argued. Still, a small part of me was scared by these arguments. The wedding arrangements had been made, though. Sam's parents and his three brothers were flying in to join 200 of my relatives and friends at our wedding. I felt there was no time to reassess the relationship.

My family and friends were all smitten by Sam after meeting him. He was charming and quick-witted, and he treated me like a queen. I was so proud that he was to be my husband. The wedding was beautiful, yet I was a little unsettled about the immensity of what it meant to be married. I had played the field for so long. Did I really want to settle down with him? What about the arguments? What about Sam's mother? I learned later that she had taken a friend of mine aside and told him she worried that I was not right for her son.

We failed to see marriage as a sacrament. When we met with the priest the day prior to our wedding, Sam and I feared he might ask us if we were living together. We considered lying, and we were relieved that he never asked. Neither of us had been to confession in many years and no one ever suggested going before the wedding. It should come as no surprise that within a couple years, it became clear that the word "holy" did not describe our marriage. We pretty much lived as non-believers, keeping God on the sidelines and relying completely on our own strength.

Sam and I returned to the West Coast after our honeymoon at the Grand Canyon. Between work and weekends spent backpacking, skiing, or beach combing, our diversions kept us busy—and happy. Though Sam was gradually growing more argumentative and impatient, the spark between us was still there.

Shortly after our second anniversary, I became pregnant. We were thrilled. We both loved babies and could not wait to have our very own. Sam came with me to every doctor's appointment and we shopped together for baby things. When our son was born, we were in awe at this miracle of life. Sam and I agreed that I would quit work and stay home full-time. I did not want to miss a minute of my son's life.

Over the next few years our relationship had its ups and downs, but gradually, the "downs" became more frequent than the "ups." Our second son was born two years later. We delighted in parenthood, but we delighted less and less in each other. Although Sam was a loving and attentive father, it was always on his terms. He was there for the fun, but the work of childcare he left mostly up to me. Whenever we had company or went anywhere, Sam considered socializing to be his job. If I made a request for help, he acted as though he couldn't hear me. If I loudly repeated my request for help, Sam would let anyone present know how irritated he was with me. Those around us had no trouble figuring out that we were not getting along.

Sam grew increasingly moody and selfish. When our third son was born in our seventh year of marriage, Sam brought me home from the hospital to a house that was a mess. He tuned me out when I asked for help and I was forced to clean the house while he sat on the porch celebrating the new baby with a cigar and a glass of whiskey. Drinking was not usually a problem for Sam, but he frequently got high on marijuana. After we had children, I asked him to stop. He refused. I also began catching Sam with pornography, but he would either play down the issue or try to cover it up.

Sam's mother increased the stress in our relationship. She regularly criticized my abilities as a wife and mother and was openly irritated with our children. Although Sam considered his mother to be a pain, he never came to my defense. "Just ignore her," was his usual response.

Since Sam could be considerate when it suited him and often surprised me with gifts, he considered himself to be a good husband. Yet, our fights had become frequent and verbally abusive. If I had any complaint, Sam tuned me out and became nasty; I usually responded with anger. Our poor little boys often heard us screaming at one another. I always felt guilty for subjecting them to this, but I lacked the self-control to stop.

When I began to threaten divorce, Sam's reaction was always, "Fine, go ahead and leave." As our relationship deteriorated, I often begged Sam to go to counseling. He refused. "All couples have problems," he would say. By the time I learned I was pregnant with our fourth child, I realized that I was in the very nightmare of a failed marriage that I had once vowed I would never find myself in. I frequently thought about leaving him, but I wondered how I would support our four children. I felt trapped.

After our fourth boy was born, I decided I needed to take birth control pills to insure we stopped having children. I did not want to bring another child into a loveless marriage. I was aware that contraception was considered a serious sin by the Catholic Church, but I didn't really care. I knew that it was wrong because it blocks a couple's God-given gift of procreation and closes them off from the possibility of life. Rather than working in union with God by using Natural Family Planning, I turned to the pill. I failed to read the fine print on the packets which explained that sometimes the pill acts as an abortifacient. It creates an environment in the womb in which a fertilized embryo cannot implant itself. Had I known this, I would not have used it.

Around this time, Sam was offered a job with a company in Minnesota. I would be closer to my family, the pay would be a little better, and we could find more affordable housing. Sam's mother made negative comments about our children growing up in some backward, provincial suburb. Her disapproval confirmed in my mind that it was the right move. Maybe getting away from her would improve things.

We settled into our new community and made friends quickly. Sam and I were as committed as ever to our children, but our marriage did not improve. While we often had good times, I always considered them just the "calm before the storm." A fight could erupt without a moment's notice, often over the pettiest of issues. After one of the many arguments when Sam left the house, I asked myself what I had done wrong.

In hindsight, the answers seemed obvious. Sam and I had planned to marry before we really even knew each other. We thought love was enough. We should have spent more time getting to know one another. Also, Sam's mother was difficult from the start. I never realized that she could affect our relationship but she definitely added strain. I didn't consider the likelihood that some of her negative traits would surface in Sam's own personality. I foolishly believed that the Sam I knew while in the thralls of romance was the *real* Sam, the Sam that would always be. I had gone into the relationship with both eyes closed.

Once in Minnesota, we limped along for another year. One evening we had a typically hateful argument. Sam stormed into another room and turned his music on loudly. When the Rolling Stones' song "Sympathy for the Devil" came on, the reality of our life sunk in. As I sat in tears, I felt as if Satan himself were laughing in my face. He was winning the battle at our house. For the first time I began to pray for our marriage: "Dear God, please help us. It could not possibly be your will that we have such a miserable marriage ... please save us ... I cannot stand it anymore. If you want me to stay in this marriage you either need to help us get better or give me the ability to accept Sam, because right now, I cannot stand this any longer."

Sam and I were not complete strangers to the Church. We occasionally went to Sunday Mass and said bedtime prayers with the kids. But God was not at the center of our lives. He was not the one I turned to or even thought of often. That slowly changed as I turned more and more to Him to save me from my misery. I finally began to realize God was my only hope.

I earnestly began reading spiritual books and learning more about my Catholic faith. Through reading the lives of the saints, I began to experience God's love. I gained powerful examples of people who had loved and served Him through difficult times. Most importantly, I began to discern between the teachings of Christ and the ways of the world.

My priorities and the way I viewed life began to change. I began praying a daily Rosary and asked the Blessed Mother to pray for our family. She is our mother in heaven. Just as at the wedding feast of Cana, she would surely go to her Son and intercede with Him about our troubles. I trusted that Jesus would not refuse His mother.

Initially, Sam resisted my newfound religious fervor. He went along to a point, but there were areas where he disagreed with me. I would pray: "Lord, you know what is best. I trust that you will handle it." Then I would regularly pray for God to guide our family and also Sam's spiritual growth.

I began to put our disagreements in God's hands. I always approached God with an openness that perhaps Sam was right and I was wrong. My prayer life strengthened significantly and it became easier for me to pull back from arguments. When my temper flared, I forced myself to pray. I never actually felt like praying at these times but I pushed through the resistance and prayed.

One of my regular prayers was for Sam to become the spiritual head of our family. Up to this point, I had single-handedly directed our children's Catholic upbringing. I also prayed for healing from all the hurt our anger and fighting had caused our children. I put my life in God's hands and asked Him to take charge. I began going to Mass during the week. If Christ was truly present at the Mass, I realized it was important for me to spend some time with Him.

As I look back, what amazes me most is that I didn't notice an improvement at first; it happened very gradually. I realized this one day in the middle of a serious argument. It occured to me that it had been a very long time since we had such a battle. I began praying, and my anger vanished within minutes and I apologized. Sam immediately apologized also, and he revealed that he had started praying too. It was as if a veil was lifted for me to see that things really were changing.

Sam began going to confession regularly. He vowed to stay away from pornography, acknowledging that it was spiritually destructive and contrary to God's will. He also made a commitment never to smoke pot again. Whenever I read a particularly inspiring book, I often asked Sam to read it as well. In time, he went from being cynical about my attending daily Mass to eventually going himself.

Because I had always wanted to improve our relationship, I had been blind to my own failings. I began to see some of my own weaknesses. My strong-willed nature had once kept me from allowing Sam to actually be the head of the family that I wanted him to be. I learned that I sometimes needed to bend my will to his. My prayers also helped me to slow my usual quick temper.

As our relationship strengthened, Sam's mother backed off. She began to see that we were a strong unit and her negative comments only hurt her relationship with her son. And finally, after much spiritual growth on both sides, we realized it was wrong to take a healthy reproductive system and alter its natural course for our own pleasure. Both of us had become open to more children. Within five years, we joyfully welcomed two more precious babies into our lives.

It has been more than ten years since our healing began. We have come a long, long way. Our older children have witnessed the power of God in the mending of our marriage. It is a lesson they will take with them through life.

Given the course of our marriage, I later wondered about its validity as a sacrament, entitled to the graces necessary to make it work. A priest explained to me that once we had gone to confession, our sacramental marriage began. We have also renewed our vows at marriage Masses.

Thankfully, we have learned that if the two of us are working towards loving and serving God, we will naturally love and serve each other. And during those times when our spouse actually becomes our cross, prayer is the answer. Sam and I have found true happiness and love. Thanks to His help, our marriage is very strong. We are proof of His healing grace.

—Anne Simpson

Anne Simpson *and her husband are raising their six children to understand the mistakes they made early in their marriage and how practicing their faith has led them to happiness. Now that some of their children are going through the teen years, they rely on their faith more than ever.*

7

All Things Are Possible

"It's over this time," I coldly told my wife over the phone. Her tears did not surprise me, but neither did they move me. "There is not going to be any counseling," I stated firmly. "We've tried it all before. We never should have been married in the first place."

Crystal was staying at my parent's house out-of-town to attend her nephew's graduation. Over the years, our marriage had experienced many highs and lows. Things would get better for a time but would always fall apart again.

While Crystal was gone, I spent some time with a female co-worker of mine in the Air Force. She was going through a divorce and I became a shoulder for her to cry on. She served the same purpose for me: I felt so comfortable talking with her that I revealed the sexual abuse I had experienced in my childhood. I had never told another soul about these experiences. Sharing such a deeply personal part of myself actually helped me form a close bond with her. It struck me that I had never felt such a closeness with Crystal. *No wonder our marriage keeps falling apart*, I decided. *We don't have what it takes to make it work. We just don't belong together.*

It would be easy for anyone to conclude that Crystal and I should never have gotten married. We met while we were just teenagers at a McDonalds where we both worked. She was seventeen and I was sixteen. Her blue eyes captivated me, but she was a year older and I assumed she was out of my league. Besides, I already had a girlfriend.

After I broke up with my girlfriend, I asked Crystal out and she accepted. On our second date, we found a remote place to park and drink beer. We also had sex. Frankly, I had little interest in her beyond the desire to use her. After that night, my respect for her diminished, not that I deserved any more respect than she. I didn't want to see her again.

Being raised Catholic I had at least a vague notion that sex outside of marriage was wrong, but my will was weak. Crystal, who had been raised in a large Lutheran family, was as rebellious as I was at the time. She also had been sexually molested at a young age. For Crystal, sex was a way to earn love and she had hoped that it would be a way for me to love her.

Six weeks later Crystal came by to talk with me. "I'm pregnant," she revealed, looking hopefully into my eyes. I was shocked. I had not given Crystal a second thought since our date.

"When are you going to have an abortion?" I asked bluntly.

Crystal took a deep breath and looked wounded. "I wasn't planning on it," she answered with tears in her eyes.

I looked at her with disgust. "I'm not going to ruin my life over a one-night stand," I announced. Despite her tears, I made it clear to her that I was not going to be trapped into marrying her. She went home and told her mother who then quickly took her for an abortion.

That summer of 1982, after my junior year of high school, I joined the Army Reserve as a way of eventually getting to college. I went away for basic training and returned home several inches taller and bulked up with muscles. Crystal made no secret of the fact that she noticed the difference in me. I was in the reserves during my senior year of high school but I still worked at McDonald's with Crystal. During a party towards the end of my senior year, she approached me and asked if we could get together. Since our last physical encounter, my spiritual faith had begun to grow and I now believed that sex was intended for marriage.

"We can go out, but I don't want us to have sex again," I told her. She made it clear that she was not interested in a non-sexual relationship. "Then we won't be getting back together," I informed her. A couple weeks later we again met at a party. This time I had been drinking and my resolve faded in the face of temptation. We had sex that night and began seeing each other regularly. By that summer, we were living together.

At the age of nineteen, I went on active duty with the Air Force and learned I would soon ship out to Okinawa, Japan. Against my father's advice, I married Crystal in my home parish on October 5, 1984. My expectation was that the love and security of marriage would make living in a foreign country easier. Instead, Crystal and I were too self-absorbed to put the other's needs first. And we did not have God to turn to because we had largely forgotten him.

We were often verbally and emotionally abusive to each other; at times, the abuse even became physical. *What have I done?* I began to ask myself. *How did I get myself trapped in this relationship?* Because of my teenage rebelliousness and refusal to listen to my father's wisdom, I felt I had made the worst mistake of my life. Nine months into the marriage, I left Crystal and began making plans to send her home. I also had a fling with another woman. *It doesn't matter, now,* I convinced myself. *This marriage is over.*

But when my sergeant learned of my plans to divorce Crystal, he strongly suggested trying marriage counseling first. "Okay, it can't hurt," I agreed. To my surprise, counseling helped us immensely. For the first time, we learned better ways of communicating rather than through fits of anger and streams of profanities.

As our relationship became a little stronger, I realized that I actually did love Crystal. Despite the guilt I carried over my adultery, I started going back to Mass. When another nine months passed and we were still happily married, Crystal and I decided to start a family. On December 29, 1986, our son, T.J., was born.

I watched in awe as a nurse bathed my new little son. When I finally was able to hold him, love and joy overwhelmed me. Then, without warning, grief stabbed at my heart. For the first time, the abortion hit me. "I put my child to death," I realized. Never before had I considered the reality of what I had done. But sadness and regret were the last things I wanted to feel on this joyous occasion. I quickly pushed away the unpleasant thought.

Initially, I brimmed with complete happiness at becoming a father. Crystal was another story: she suffered from intense post-partum depression. It never occurred to me at the time, but she was also grieving her abortion. Her physical and emotional burdens exacerbated this depression. At first, I willingly cared for both Crystal and my new son. But as the weeks passed and she continued to be sullen and uninterested in either me or the baby, I began to resent her.

Several months passed, and Crystal returned to work but remained depressed. I started to feel like a single parent. She was not really a part of either my life or our baby's life. My son's babysitter adored him, however. *Why can't his own mother appreciate him like this?* I often wondered angrily. Seeing T.J.'s face light up when I picked him up at the babysitter's house became the highlight of my day. But soon, seeing the babysitter's face light up when she saw *me* became equally exciting. What started out as sharing an appreciation for my son soon turned into flirting and an attraction for each other. An affair soon began.

During this time, in June of 1987, we came home from Okinawa so I could be the best man in a friend's wedding. It was held in the same church in which Crystal and I were married. During the ceremony, I realized that the vows being exchanged were not just a commitment between two people but to God as well. I knew I had not just betrayed Crystal but God, too. On the spot I repented of my sin and vowed to live a faithful covenant with my bride. I did not yet grasp my need to go to confession as a way of healing my soul, which had been deadened by such a grave sin.

Although I had committed to being a better husband, I did not understand the concept of including Christ as the third person of our union. But, at least for a time, it seemed we were getting back on the right track. Crystal's depression lifted. She had begun taking better care of herself and shed the extra weight remaining from her pregnancy. She had also grown to love motherhood. It looked like we might make things work after all.

I was transferred back to Texas in October of 1987 and started working on a college degree at Wayland Baptist University. Classes in Old and New Testament history were required to earn a degree. It was really the first time in my life that I had opened a Bible and read it. I developed a prayer life too, but I still had a long way to go. My prayers centered around me and my desires. I failed to see that I should have been praying for my will to be conformed to God's will. Not surprisingly, it was not long before our marriage floundered again, and I again strayed. Being involved in a third adulterous affair made me believe that I would never be able to remain faithful to Crystal for very long. I let her know that I did not see any hope for our marriage. Crystal was deeply hurt but she, too, was at a loss as to how to make things better. We separated, but she let me know that it was not what she wanted.

An uncle who was a devout Catholic learned of our plans to divorce and pleaded with us to give the marriage one more chance. He convinced us to attend a *Discovering Anew* weekend through the Diocese of Dallas as part of the Retrouvaille program for troubled marriages. I ended my affair and agreed to give the marriage one last shot.

The weekend was God-inspired. For the first time, I learned how our backgrounds affected the people we were and the way we responded to one another as husband and wife. I realized that the deep wounds from the sexual abuse of my early childhood manifested itself in my affairs. If healing were to come, I could not rely on my own strength. I finally recognized my need for the sacrament of Reconciliation, and I went to confession for the first time in many years. I felt healed and ready to return to our marriage fully committed.

In the beginning, Crystal and I worked hard to keep the communication going. Before long, though, we closed our "tool box" and reverted back to old patterns. All the discoveries and new behaviors that had renewed our relationship went by the wayside. At this time, I was working two jobs and attending college which zapped me of my time and energy. Crystal resented that I had no time in my life for her. Again, we pulled in different directions. It was at this time that Crystal left to attend her nephew's graduation and I spent time talking with a coworker, Gloria (not her real name). The special "bond" I thought I felt with Gloria— the type of bond I never felt with Crystal—seemed reason enough to face up to the fact that Crystal and I did not belong together. I talked to a priest on the base about my desire to divorce. He did not try to stop me but instead advised that I file for an annulment. It was all the confirmation I needed.

It was cowardly of me to break the news to Crystal over the phone. But with Gloria in the wings now, I wanted to disassociate myself from Crystal as quickly as possible. I knew it would hurt her, but my concern was for myself. By telling her over the phone, I hoped an emotional scene could be avoided. Crystal did not handle it well. Even though she, too, was often frustrated with our relationship, she really wanted us to stay together. Her tears and pleas failed to move me. As far as I was concerned, the sooner we went our separate ways, the better off we would both be. I was convinced that together we would only bring each other misery.

In September of 1991, with the divorce final, I was ready to start my new life without Crystal. A mere two months after the divorce, Gloria and I married. She was Pentecostal but expressed a desire to become Catholic. I learned that we both needed to get our marriages annulled. What I ignored was the fact that in the eyes of the Church, I was still married to Crystal.

I learned later that even after we divorced, Crystal had prayed fervently for a reconciliation. Once I was remarried though, she gave up hope. A year later, Crystal had also remarried. That was fine with me. Gloria and I had retired from the military and had good jobs, a new house, and a new truck and van. We told ourselves we were so blessed. From my point of view, life had never been better. But soon, our perfect life began to fall apart. First, I lost my job. Then, since we could not keep up with the mortgage payments, we lost our house. The financial stress and feeling of failure led to a deep depression. I did not understand how everything had unraveled so quickly. I knew something was terribly wrong, but I did not know what I was supposed to do. Finally, I called out to God in prayer. I was ready to humble myself. It became clear to me that I really did not know what I wanted or what was best for me. I acknowledged that I was not in control; God was. In desperation, I asked for His will—not mine—to be done in my life.

For several months I continued to pray and plead for God to show me the way. Then, at the beginning of Lent of 1994, I made a vow to read my Bible daily. It was at this time that I had a deep spiritual experience. I felt the Holy Spirit opening my eyes, giving me the wisdom to follow Christ—to do things His way, not mine. It was a profound experience that left me feeling peaceful and ready to empty myself of self-love and fill up with God's love. That day, my whole life changed. From that point on, I began reading and learning about my faith and accepted the teachings of the Catholic Church. Another woman also came into my life at that time: the Blessed Mother. I came to understand that Jesus' words from the Cross, "Behold your Mother," were meant for all of us. Mary, the woman through whom Jesus came to us, longed to lead me closer to her Son.

I began praying all fifteen decades of the Rosary, attending daily Mass as often as I could, reading my Bible, fasting twice a week, and trying to live each moment in the presence of God. Because of this deep conversion, I soon realized that Gloria and I were not truly married in God's eyes. The special bond I thought we had shared seemed like nothing now. It was my sacramental commitment to Crystal in the bond of matrimony that mattered. By the end of Lent, I knew that I had to end my relationship with Gloria and ask for Crystal's forgiveness for divorcing her. Thankfully, at this time, Gloria was coming to the same conclusion that I was. She too desired reconciliation with her ex-husband.

The thought of laying this all before Crystal was frightening. *What will I say? Where should I begin? How am I going to get time alone with her?* I wondered. I nervously put it off for several weeks until one weekend an opportunity to be alone with Crystal presented itself. Her husband was home sick, so she had joined me alone to watch one of T.J.'s soccer games.

Praying for the right words, I took a deep breath and looked into her blue eyes. "Crystal," I began. "I'm so sorry. I never should have divorced you. I know what I did was wrong and I am open to reconciliation."

Crystal stared back at me in utter surprise. She took a moment to let my words sink in. "I forgive you," she whispered. Nothing more was said at that time. I felt a powerful love for Crystal and it hurt to think I had pushed her into the arms of another man. But there was nothing more I could do now, except to continue praying for God's will. A few days later, Crystal revealed to me that she too was unhappy with her second marriage. She admitted marrying out of a sense of loneliness when all along she still felt that we belonged together.

In a short time, we divorced our second spouses as sensitively as we could and asked a priest how Crystal and I should reconcile. The priest explained we should go to confession but could begin living as husband and wife immediately since we were still married in the eyes of God.

One of the happiest aspects of our reconciliation was sharing the news with our son. T.J. was ecstatic when he learned his mom and dad would be together again. "I'm so happy," he gushed when I told him the wonderful news. We still had our original wedding bands so we placed them on each other's fingers again and promised a lifetime of commitment to one another.

Life fell into place right away. Shortly after our reconciliation, I was offered a job that provided a good enough income to allow Crystal to be a full-time wife and mother which is what we both desired. Together, we were growing in the Catholic faith. Crystal enrolled in the RCIA program and was confirmed at Easter in 1995. During Crystal's time of preparation, we came to understand the Church's teaching on sexuality in marriage. Crystal had a tubal ligation during her remarriage, and I had gotten a vasectomy shortly after T.J.'s birth. Because of our desire to fully live out our faith, we both began to regret these decisions.

During confession one day, I talked to a priest about my sterilization. The priest told me I should have it reversed. I did not even tell him about Crystal's sterilization. I thought about the priest's advice but hesitated when I considered the financial cost. Still, the issue unsettled me. Through prayer and a discussion with a second priest, the desire grew within me to undergo a reversal. The Catholic Church did not demand that I do this but I wanted nothing to stand in the way of opening myself up to God's will for me. I went into surgery with my rosary and complete peace in the depths of my soul.

The Lord began to work on Crystal's heart too. She started to desire more children without any prodding from me whatsoever. A year after I had my reversal done, Crystal also went through the reversal process. I was in the waiting room after the surgery. The doctor came in looking grim. He told me that one of Crystal's ovaries had been destroyed by a benign cyst. After connecting the fallopian tubes, they discovered that both tubes were blocked at the uterine wall.

I was disappointed, but my heart broke for Crystal. She had begun looking forward to having more children. I knew I would be content with one child, but now I worried that the news would hurt Crystal terribly. When she returned to the room, I explained the situation. To my surprise, she smiled gently. "That's OK," she said quietly. "It was the right thing to do. It's in God's hands now." I had never seen her glow with such grace and beauty.

It has been eleven years since Crystal and I reconciled. I'm currently working on a masters degree in marriage and family counseling, so the burden of both work and school is upon me again. In the past, our relationship faltered under such stress, but everything is different now. Our marriage is about more than just love. It is a life-long covenant between us and God. At times there is still anger between us, but we have learned to turn to God in such moments. We have also learned to avoid the destructive choices of the past. Instead, even when I'm angry with Crystal, I know that I still love her. That's when I pray, "Lord, touch my heart and help me to know what to do to make this relationship better. Fill my heart with what I need to be the husband and father I need to be." I also pray for Crystal—not for her to change but for God to guide her to be the wife and mother He has called her to be.

My strength now comes from frequent attendance at Mass and Eucharistic adoration. Through these gifts, I open myself up to all God's graces. I also count on the Blessed Mother at my side to keep me close to her son, Jesus. One of my greatest joys is that Crystal too is very devoted to the faith we now share.

I'm convinced that we will never let our relationship spin out of control again. We have learned that there is no real happiness except through God. We have learned that a marriage takes three: husband, wife, and Christ, to seal the covenant with His Blood. Through Him, all things are possible. We are certainly proof of that.

—James DePiazza

8

From Darkness to Light

As I sat in my in-laws' house, I wondered how I could ever get out of the mess I had created. Pornography had become a monster in my life. I was absolutely addicted and it was causing unbelievable pain to Michelle, my wife of thirteen years. I was amazed that we were still together. It was September 2002, and we had just moved back to Tulsa, Oklahoma, to try to make a new start. But in my heart I had lost all hope. I knew she would eventually be fed up with my selfishness and my habitual use of pornography. I wanted to leave it behind, but I didn't know if I ever could. I didn't know how.

For the most part Michelle and I were able to live a normal life, at least outwardly. At home, though, it was a different story. From the beginning of our relationship there were signs of impending problems that threatened to destroy us. We had met in October 1985 at an Oklahoma "New Wave" nightclub where I spent a lot of time. I was at a low point in my life, feeling empty because of all the casual sexual encounters I'd had that summer. To add to my problems, I'd been indulging in pornographic magazines and losing myself in fantasy since I was twelve. I can attest that pornography, like drugs, creates a downward spiral that ultimately leaves a person unsatisfied and filled with despair.

I was lost. God was not a part of my life; I had no relationship with Him whatsoever. Sometimes I would cry out to Him in desperation, as I did one day in the fall of 1985. Overcome by a feeling of intense emptiness, I asked

God to show me my life's purpose and for someone to fill the hollowness.

Shortly thereafter, I met Michelle. She was everything I had ever dreamed about—beautiful, smart, fun, a deep thinker. She was the answer to my prayers. Michelle was a cradle Catholic and the oldest daughter of a good family. I had previously been in a couple of semi-serious relationships that ended in disappointment. I could tell, though, that Michelle was different. But I was a wounded soul, and after the first few romance-filled months, I reverted to my selfish ways.

I yearned to use my creative talents as an artist, but I had dropped out of a degree program in graphic arts and had difficulty keeping a job. I was also irresponsible with money. I decided to leave Oklahoma and study fashion design at a school in southern California. Though Michelle and I carried on a long-distance relationship, I found more temptation in California to feed my growing addiction to pornography. It was everywhere, especially in Hollywood, where I got a part-time job working at a trendy clothing store on Melrose Avenue. Because of the way I dressed and looked, I fit right in. My ego grew as I became popular for the first time in my life.

Michelle came to live with me during her summer vacation and even loaned me money. But I was unhappy and, after less than a year, I returned to Oklahoma. After a fruitless job search, I decided to join the military.

In December 1986, I enlisted in the Air Force for a six-year term and was stationed in California. Michelle and I continued our relationship while she remained in Tulsa to finish college. While in the Air Force I excelled in my job as a graphic artist. But my living situation was a breeding ground for sin. Virtually every weekend was filled with partying, alcohol, and women. My addiction to pornography got worse.

Michelle finished college during my third year in the military, and we decided to get married. Our marriage seemed destined for failure from the start because my understanding of women was deeply skewed by the sexual fanatsies I indulged in. I had no clue what it meant to be a good husband.

I flew to Tulsa for our "storybook" wedding at the Holy Family Cathedral. Not being Catholic, I really didn't understand what the ceremony was all about. Nor did I understand the uniqueness of the Catholic Church. To me, one church was just as good as another. But Michelle was Catholic and wanted to get married there, so it was fine with me.

After we were married, Michelle moved to California with me and got a job as an elementary school teacher. It didn't take long for the battle taking place in my soul to start affecting our marriage. I racked up big phone bills with dial-a-porn services and regularly purchased "adult" magazines. When Michelle confronted me about the bills and magazines, I lied or played them down. This became the cycle of our lives. I had been pulled into a black hole and felt unable to climb up out of it.

At the time, I couldn't see how truly poisonous pornography is. I didn't realize how it turns a man inward and makes him selfish. It causes men to see women as little more than objects. Many problems arise if a man pursues and marries a woman on this basis. He doesn't love her for the unique person she is, but for some physical qualities she possesses. So when age and gravity take their toll, he will no longer find her attractive and can easily justify leaving her to find another woman with the physical features he seeks.

Because pornography denigrates the extraordinary mystery of sex (which is actually a profound foreshadowing of the union we will experience in the Beatific Vision in heaven), marital intimacy becomes an act of self-gratification rather than self-donation. Porn also stifles one's ability to communicate. A woman who respects herself will ultimately recoil when she realizes she is not being loved as a person, but rather as a sexual object.

Michelle, having grown tired of feeling used and thinking that deepening our faith would help our marriage, suggested we attend a Catholic Church near our home in Riverside, California. Soon, I decided that maybe I should become a Catholic. I didn't have any reasons for joining the Church, other than I thought maybe it would help me spiritually. I went through the Rite of Christian Initiation for Adults (RCIA) and was accepted into the Church on Easter 1991. In retrospect, I realize I learned very little about the truths of the Faith. With such a weak foundation in the moral teachings of the Church, it is no surprise we stopped going to Mass after a few years.

During this time I finished my term in the Air Force and started a home-based freelance graphics business. But I was undisciplined and distracted, especially now that we had a computer bringing Internet pornography into our house. Michelle became the primary breadwinner, which put additional pressure on our already strained marriage.

With our debt mounting, I took a full-time graphic artist job with a local public transportation agency. Now I had access to Internet porn at work and home. By this point, I had rejected "organized religion," which for me meant Catholicism. I also turned down several Protestant acquaintances who invited me to church. To me, perhaps because of my sick psyche, they came off as self-righteous.

I resolved to do things my way. I began researching my family history and became fascinated by the ancient beliefs of my ancestors. Being of Scottish and Irish descent, I was drawn to the ancient Celts' pagan beliefs, ignoring the fact that they were Christians for the majority of Celtic history. I was convinced that paganism was the answer. I was going to revive the ancient customs that I believed had been extinguished by Christianity. So I fully embraced paganism, worshipping many gods through prayer, meditation, and guided imagery. I had my patron deities, all based on ancient Irish deities. I created rituals that marked specific events such as the first day of spring or birthdays. Then I honored the gods and goddesses associated with that occasion. I continued these practices for several years, dragging Michelle along with me.

Then, in 1997, I lost my job, mainly because I wasn't disciplined enough and regularly viewed porn on my computer at work. Despite my unemployment, Michelle and I went on a long-planned vacation to Scotland, where we experienced a renewed love for each other. During this three-week trip, we decided to start a family.

When my son was born a year later, I was in absolute awe. I tried to be a good father, but I was not ready for fatherhood. I thought being a father would help fill that sense of incompleteness that I was feeling. Deep down, though, I was afraid that I would not be a good father, that I would somehow fail at that just as I'd failed at everything I chased to find a purpose for my life.

I decided to pursue a degree in medieval European history, and this led me to enroll in a study-abroad program in Scotland. Leaving behind Michelle and our seven-month-old son, I began my studies there in September of 1999, filled with ambition. But I ended up spending much of my year abroad engrossed in my addiction to Internet pornography, frequently skipping classes.

I returned home and told Michelle that I failed to complete my courses mainly because of my porn addiction. She was devastated. She had finally had enough. She was filled with anger and pain, and rightly so. Following a particularly bad argument, Michelle called an intervention meeting of a few of our close friends. As a result of this meeting, she served me with an ultimatum—either I seek psychological help or she would file for divorce. I had no choice; the next day I went to a psychiatrist who diagnosed me as having bipolar disorder.

Relieved we had found a solution, I started medication and began counseling. Though I was convinced I should remain a pagan, we decided to go back to church for the sake of our son. But I wanted nothing to do with the Catholic Church, which I identified as "the ultimate organized religion." So we found a Presbyterian church, which I found less offensive to my self-dominated worldview. Though I was a confirmed pagan, I found that I could tolerate the Presbyterian Church. In fact, many in that church had no problems with my pagan views and even willingly participated in my "rituals" at times.

Since it looked like I was making progress with my psychological issues, we decided to have another child. Our daughter was born in November 2001, and we moved back to Tulsa the next summer. We wanted to escape California for many reasons—the many bad memories, the state's materialistic culture, its overcrowding. We moved in with Michelle's parents, and Michelle stayed at home with the kids while I looked for a job.

After a few months, I became discouraged with my job search. I was feeling hopeless and afraid. As I had done at other critical times, I called out to God, even though I was no longer sure of His existence. "God," I prayed, "I'm not sure what to believe anymore. If you really exist, then please help me. I need a job. Please help me to put my life right. If you do this for me, I will give my life to you."

Not long afterward, I landed a job as a graphic designer for a major car rental company. Soon after, we found a home. Things were finally falling into place. Of course I had conveniently forgotten about my earlier prayer. But God remembered—and He was going to hold me to my word.

A few weeks later, Michelle's mother gave us two tickets to a marriage seminar presented by an evangelical Christian family movement. Michelle and I agreed to go, but we didn't know what to expect. Throughout the day, I came to realize what a horribly selfish person I was and how this, coupled with my pornography addiction, was the primary cause of our marital problems. I realized what a mess I had made of my life. But I didn't know how I was going to fix it or how I could possibly atone for all the pain I had caused Michelle.

At the end of the seminar, the presenters offered a rose to all who were attending if they felt they needed God's forgiveness. I still wasn't convinced God existed, but I immediately got up. Michelle thought I was going to get the rose as a gift to give to her. But I told her, "It's not for you; it's for me. I need forgiveness."

I made my way down to the floor of the civic center and took my place in a long line of those seeking God's forgiveness. Oblivious to the crowd, I began reflecting on all the sinful things I had done in my life, all the ways I had failed as a husband and father.

What happened next I can only describe as a supernatural experience. As I stood there, I felt an all-consuming presence come over me. I was overshadowed by something so big that I felt as if I didn't even exist. In my mind I asked, *Is that you, God?*

And His answer came back, very clearly. *Yes!*

I felt as if He was saying, *Welcome back. I'm so happy you have finally come back home.* I broke into tears. I was back in the arms of the Lord! The prodigal son had returned. To this day, whenever I think of that experience, I break into tears. I stood there sobbing before eventually receiving my rose. I promptly returned to my seat and embraced Michelle. We both sat and wept. I felt so truly sorry for the hurt I had caused her. But I didn't say anything about what I had just experienced because I wasn't sure how to tell her or if she would even believe me. I didn't know if I could believe it myself.

For several weeks I pondered what had happened. Was I still pagan? Or was I now a Christian? After some deep reflection and prayer, I knew that I had to reject my pagan beliefs and embrace the one true God. When we had gone back to our Presbyterian church in Tulsa, I attended with a renewed love and appreciation for God. I also began to pray to God daily for the first time in my life. One of the first things I asked Him was, *What do you want me to do?* He told me, *Be the best husband and father you can possibly be.* When I asked how I was to accomplish this, He told me to trust in Him. So I gave Him my heart and for the first time I began to sense peace in my life. I also felt an overwhelming urge to read the Bible. I asked God where He wanted me to go, physically and spiritually. Initially, I just wanted to know more about who God is and what His plan for my life was. I was open to His lead. I had made a complete mess of my life so I gave Him control. I felt the urging to search for answers.

If I was going to be a Christian, then I wanted to give it my all and do His will.

As I began studying history, I was amazed to discover that there had been only one Christian church for 1,500 years—the Catholic Church—and that the thousands of Protestant denominations had only sprung up only in last 500 years.

This didn't seem right to me. In prayer, I asked God again, *What is the truth? Does it matter anyway?* I knew, though, that I needed to continue my search.

Throughout this time, I prayed a simple prayer all day long. It's called the Jesus Prayer: "Lord Jesus Christ, son of God, have mercy on me, a sinner." I must have prayed it a hundred times a day.

I continued to search, but I didn't know what to think. If the Bible is the only thing necessary to know the truth, then why are there so many interpretations of it? If the Holy Spirit guides each person in the correct interpretation of the Word, then why doesn't every Christian believe the same things? Why are there so many different denominations?

I approached my search for Truth like a detective. I knew that if two lawyers disagreed about the interpretation of a law, they would go to the earliest use of that law to see how it was originally interpreted. I decided to do the same.

I needed to go back to where it all began. I knew I had to rely on primary sources. I went back to the writings of the early Church fathers, the Christian leaders who lived and wrote during the first centuries of the Faith. Surely, I thought, they would profess what Jesus truly taught because they lived so soon after the establishment of the Church.

As I read the Bible and studied the writings of the Church fathers, the truth gradually emerged. I came to realize that only a few of today's churches look anything like the churches of the first centuries of Christianity. I looked closely at the church described in the Book of Acts, and compared this with the church described by St. Irenaeus in the second century. I also read the descriptions of Sts. Justin Martyr, Clement of Rome, and Polycarp of Smyrna, Church fathers who lived in the first, second, and third centuries.

I eventually concluded that only two churches fit the model of the early church: the Eastern Orthodox and the Catholic Church. As I started to compare the two, I discovered that each claims to be the "original" church, and that there are many remarkable similarities between them: each hold to Sacred Tradition, apostolic succession, seven sacraments, devotion to Mary, the communion of saints, and other similar beliefs. Because of my past prejudices against the Catholic Church, though, I began to lean toward Orthodoxy.

The more research I did, however, the more the truth became clear. I found that the Orthodox Church has changed some of its teachings over the centuries, whereas the Catholic Church has held fast to its beliefs. Through twenty-one major Church councils and hundreds of declarations by the popes, no doctrines contradicted earlier teachings. I found this amazing. How could a church not change its teachings in 2,000 years? How was this possible? To me, this was a clear indication of the truth of the Catholic Church. As I came to this conclusion, I asked God, *Is this it? Is this where the truth can be found?*

The answer came to me in my reading of the Bible. I saw that Christ instructed the Church to preach everything He taught (Mt 28:19-20), and He had promised the protection of the Holy Spirit to "guide [the Church] into all the truth" (Jn 16:13). If the Church had changed any of His teachings, then

Jesus would be a liar. He taught that even though individual members of the Church might sin, He would preserve the Church in truth until the end of time.

On February 2, 2003, I told Michelle that we needed to return to the Catholic Church. She looked at me as if I were crazy. I then told her all that had been happening in my life: how God had made Himself known to me, my conversion, the research, and what I had discovered as a result. She agreed to attend Mass with me the following Sunday. That Saturday, I felt an incredible urge to go to confession. I knew that before I could truly be reconciled with God, I needed the sacrament of Penance. I wanted to receive Jesus in the Eucharist—body, blood, soul, and divinity—but I first needed to be cleansed of my sins.

I called the pastor of the local parish, asking if I could go to confession. I told him that I had been to confession only once, twelve years earlier, when I first entered the Catholic Church. At that time I'd avoided confessing anything of real substance, including my porn addiction. This time, though, I told the priest everything I had ever done. I was with him for over an hour. When I left his office, I felt like a new person. I was overcome by an incredible sense of peace, the same peace I'd experienced at the marriage retreat. Everything had been made new again—my life, my marriage, and my heart.

The first Sunday we went to Mass, I cried. I was home and a new life had just begun. I had found everything I had been searching for. I knew the purpose and meaning of my life, but most of all, I had someone to fill the emptiness I had been feeling: Jesus Christ. He took away my addiction because I gave Him my heart. I had started praying the Rosary almost daily, then began a weekly hour of Eucharistic adoration. During these hours I experienced deep healing and discovered a profound sense of peace in my life. Soon, I was attending daily Mass. I learned that by giving myself to Jesus, He gave me back my life.

I have experienced a radical change in my understanding of women. What pornography had destroyed, Jesus has healed. Before this, I was unable to truly communicate with my wife because I was so self-absorbed. I saw sex as a means to personal fulfillment instead of understanding the words of St. Thomas Aquinas that "to love is to will the greater good of another."

An addiction becomes the number one thing in your life, even when you are trying to be a good husband and father. You will do anything to get your "fix," even risking your life and relationships. The more you indulge, the more twisted your concept of human relations becomes.

I now have extended periods when I'm not tempted by pornography. But then I am besieged by temptation. I notice these temptations usually increase when I am about to do something that is directly opposed to porn addiction, such as giving a talk to men about the dangers of pornography. But I get through these periods of temptation through prayer and the sacraments, and I am able to resist them with the help of God's grace.

I can do all things in Him.

—Kenneth Henderson

Kenneth Henderson *is the founder of the True Knights apostolate (www. trueknights.org). Its mission calls men to be the best husbands, fathers, and sons that they be in the eyes of God, with a special mission of helping men break free of pornography addiction. Ken regularly speaks on this subject as well as on other Catholic family life and apologetics topics. For more information, call (512) 684-0767, e-mail ken.henderson@trueknights.org, or visit www.trueknights.org.*

9

Trading Earthly Treasures
for Heavenly Ones

Genie's story:

I remember thinking, "Everyone thinks our life is truly envious, they think we have it all." But the ache in my heart said, "We are losing everything. All we have is emptiness."

Frank was a successful young attorney and the assistant district attorney for our county. I was a journalist. We ran in the "right" social circles. We had no lack of money, prestige, or comforts. Yet, our marriage was in shambles.

"We need a divorce." I told myself. "It's the only way out."

Then, overnight, everything changed. Jesus offered us a "way out." He rescued us from disaster. The rescue was so dramatic that in less than a year, we sold all we owned and became missionaries in third world countries. To our friends, family, and people in our community, it looked like we had given up everything. As I look back, remembering how it all started, I am still amazed at the treasure we found.

Frank and I were young when we married. Circumstances had moved us to a serious relationship. I had been so much in love, it was crazy that it wasn't working out.

In 1961, when I arrived at Louisiana State University's summer semester to get an early start on my future, I had the world by the tail—or so I thought. I had grown up in a strong, loving, and socially-prominent Catholic family. My plan was to become a doctor. During my freshman year, I was nominated and elected to the LSU beauty court, but my world soon came crashing down on me when I became pregnant outside of marriage that same year. The surrender of my beautiful son was totally sobering. There is a primal wound for both mom and baby that really never heals.

I spent the final part of my pregnancy at St. Anthony's Infant Home, so no one except very close family even learned of it. My precious son was born on March 26, 1962. I held him tightly to my breast and whispered, "Don't be afraid. I'll always love you. I will always pray for you. I will never forget you." I prayed that my baby would go to a loving home with both a mother and a father to care for him. The social consensus in the early 1960s was that "unwed" mothers were "unfit" mothers. I was convinced that adoption would provide the happiness and security for him that I could not.

Almost overnight, I lost all desire to become a doctor. Instead, I prayed to St. Anthony to help me find a good husband and live happily ever after. Once I had assurance that my baby son had gone to a loving home, I regained strength and enthusiasm for life. That summer I was accepted into a nursing school in New Orleans.

On the Saturday of Memorial Day weekend, I received a phone call. As soon as I realized it was Frank Summers on the line, my heart pounded wildly.

"Frank, what a surprise!" I exclaimed. "It's been two years since you left Abbeville, right?"

During our high school years at Mt. Carmel High, I had a secret crush on Frank. My rival for his affection in those days, however, was totally out of my league. Frank was head over heels in love—with the great outdoors.

Frank's family had moved away to New Orleans after his father became a Louisiana Supreme Court justice. (He would later be named the Court's chief justice.) I learned that Frank was staying in Abbeville with his grandmother and taking summer classes at the local university. In the fall, he would be a junior majoring in English and planning for law school. We'd both be attending school in New Orleans.

"I wondered," Frank asked, "if you'd like to go to a movie with me next Saturday night?"

"I don't think I have any plans yet, so I think it would be fun," I said, trying not to sound overly anxious.

After our first date, I could not contain my excitement. When I got home, I ran to Mama and Daddy's room to tell them about this man that God had sent me. I was sure I could never marry anyone more wonderful than Frank Summers.

Our courtship that summer and into the school year was like a fairy tale. As our love story progressed, I realized I needed to tell Frank about my baby. So, one day, as we sat on a Lake Pontchartrain seawall watching sailboats, I revealed my secret. I looked into his eyes and saw pain. He expressed sorrow that the girl he loved had undergone that kind of suffering. My heart melted as Frank then told me he loved me and wanted us to grow old together. He confessed that he had come to Abbeville the previous summer intending for us to date and ultimately marry.

When Frank's parents advised us to wait until he finished law school, we decided to elope and were married by a probate judge on May 11, 1963. I was nineteen and Frank was twenty. Although Frank had been drifting from his Catholic faith, on our wedding night he held both my hands and said, "Let's kneel down and thank God for our marriage." We knelt and Frank prayed, "Thank you, God for my beautiful, beautiful wife." My eyes filled with tears of joy.

Two months later, we were married in the Catholic Church and again made a commitment to one another before God and family. The following fall, Frank started law school at Tulane University in New Orleans. We lived in a servant's cottage behind his parents' elegant three-story home. Since the nursing school did not accept married students at that time, I took a job with the accounting department at the university. Although we lived on a shoestring budget, it seemed love was all we needed. Both of us soon yearned to start a family. A month after our first anniversary, our beautiful baby boy was born. We named him Frank Wynerth Summers III, but called him by the nickname Beau. He filled our hearts with love and hope. God had been good to us, but unfortunately we did not think about Him much anymore.

Shortly after we married, Frank stopped attending Mass. It was not long before I, too, gave in to leisurely Sunday mornings and neglected God and church. As the honeymoon faded into routine, our differences in temperament began to show. Most obviously, I was gregarious and talkative, while Frank was quiet and a loner. As the rigors of married life encroached on our earlier romantic notions, tension, resentment, and distrust began to eat away at our unity.

In retrospect, this was a time we really needed God to anchor our family. Instead, we turned to partying, which led to fights about drinking and flirting. We loved each other, but the alcohol and socializing were like an acid eroding the foundation of our marriage.

After Frank graduated from law school, he decided to further his legal education with some post-graduate work in London. Planning for this exotic trip became a balm that soothed our wounded marriage. Frank clerked for a judge for two years while we saved up for our year in London. During this time, I also returned to school, majoring in English literature. I kept a 4.0 average, cared for Beau, and still managed to be part of the social scene.

Our adventure in London was everything we dreamed it would be. We lived in Soho, in a fourth floor apartment. The theater district, Piccadilly Circus, and Green Park were practically at our doorstep. Beau made friends with Trafalgar Square's pigeons, and we came to know our way around the National Museum. Most importantly, our marriage grew strong. Stepping out of our world and into a new one caused us to cling together.

After fourteen months it was time to return home. When Frank saw my tears one night, he asked why I was crying.

"I'm just worried that we won't be able to hang on to the closeness," I said, wiping my eyes.

"We'll just have to work at it, Babe," he answered.

Before we were even unpacked, friends started calling. As usual, we mixed a few drinks and went out to celebrate. I felt a flush of pleasure when some men greeted my new outfit and false eyelashes with catcalls. That night, as I flirted and enjoyed all the attention, Frank spent time visiting with an acquaintance of ours whose husband was not there.

Suddenly, it hit me that we had fallen right into our same old destructive pattern barely one week after returning. Tears streamed down my face, weakening the glue on my false eyelashes. As I gingerly tucked them into my pocket, it occurred to me that my superficial life was also coming unglued. I felt despair, which only deepened as Frank and I drifted apart.

He began practicing law during the week and spent his weekends hunting and fishing. Meanwhile, I found company with single or divorced girlfriends. Emptiness and bitterness again became part of both our lives. When Frank came home from work one evening and announced he wanted to get a doctorate at Columbia Law School in New York, the idea captivated us both. Perhaps we could recapture some of the magic of experiencing a new place together again.

Sure enough, New York seemed to be just what we needed. We took in all the free entertainment at Lincoln Center and in Central Park and made an interesting assortment of friends with international backgrounds. During this time, I was introduced to women's liberation and embraced militant feminist propaganda. It seemed to me that all the exposure to different people and philosophies gave us a new dimension in sophistication.

After Frank received his doctorate, we returned to Louisiana in May 1972, and he entered private practice. Within a few months of our arrival, he was appointed assistant district attorney. We found the right house, bought a new car, and enrolled Beau in Mt. Carmel elementary school, which Frank and I had attended as children.

But as we re-entered our previous whirlwind lifestyle, the old strains on our marriage returned with a vengeance. Our love was strangled by too much drinking and too many outside pressures; our lives took us in indifferent directions. I worked as a society editor and later as the director of a self-help housing program. I was traveling and growing independent. Beau spent a lot of time with his grandparents.

Our public fights gave testimony to our crumbling marriage. Only later did I learn that friends and family were praying for us, rigorously. My parents were pained to see how we neglected God. Frank's cynicism and critical arguments against the Catholic Church—or any church for that matter—made his atheism just as public.

We were miserable, but we could not stop hurting one another. I decided to visit my recently divorced cousin in Houston. I took nine-year-old Beau with me on what was really a "scouting" trip, since I planned to take him and join my cousin after I divorced Frank.

My cousin, from her perspective as a divorcée, tried to dissuade me when I disclosed my desire to leave Frank. I considered her opinion. *No*, I thought. *This is for the best. There are so many things that Frank and I cannot talk about. He has frozen me out of his life. We live in a cold silence that is only broken with drinking and shouting matches. I had promised myself I would never do this, but I can't stop. I have to get away from Frank.*

When Beau and I returned home and pulled into the driveway, I was relieved to see all the lights out. *Good*, I thought. *We can put off until tomorrow our final fight—the one where I declare the death of our marriage and the imminence of our divorce.*

Frank was asleep on the sofa. Beau drowsily went to his room while I tiptoed into bed. Just as I was about to turn off the light, Frank walked into the room. He smiled. I was totally disarmed. Frank looked so different. This was not the man I had left a few days earlier.

"I have something to read to you," he said. "Why don't you come and sit by me?"

His voice was loving and tender. Frank then proceeded to read a seven-page letter to me. He began by asking for my forgiveness for the many ways in which he had failed as a husband and father. He took upon his shoulders the responsibility for the state of our marriage. As head of the house, he was responsible. Next, he forgave me for all my sins against him—really forgave me.

"I love you," he read on. "We can try again. This time we can make it." So many healing and hopeful things were said in the letter. I was transfixed. There was an unfamiliar aura of peace around us. He ended his letter by saying, "The Lord Jesus will help us rebuild our marriage. We'll try to keep the Lord's Day holy by starting with going to church on Sunday. God will help us."

My mind could not grasp what Frank was saying. *God will help us? Frank had denied God for so long. What could have possibility gotten into him? What made you say the Lord will help us?* I wanted to know.

I was totally unprepared for the story Frank told me.

"I was alone but not enjoying my solitude," he began. "The realization of our marriage breakup shook me. At first I thought, 'Good riddance, I'll be free to live my life in peace. I'll meet a prettier woman.' But I was in pain and I didn't want to lose Beau, either.

"Tonight, I asked myself, 'Where is the "happily ever after"? I followed all the formulas for success, but what good is all the money? So what?' The futility of it all was crushing. Despair swallowed me. I was seated on the sofa and began to cry. Genie, you've never seen me weep like that. I was really weeping for the first time in my adult life. I thought of suicide. I almost got up to get my pistol, but then I couldn't bear to think of the shame that it would cause Beau.

"In my crying I suddenly had a strong sense that I was no longer alone. Someone else was there with me. I sat up straight and dried my eyes. I was ashamed that someone might see me crying. I looked around. I was alone. No one else was there.

"I began weeping again when suddenly, that presence was there again. This time it was much more powerful and nearer. I felt that I could reach out and touch it.

"It was God. I knew it was God! My despair washed away as the presence of Almighty God surrounded me. It actually flowed into me. God had come to me in my loneliest hour.

"Instinctively, I knew that the presence of God was not there to punish me. Instead, I felt an incredible flood of love. Again, I wondered why. I had not been praying or looking for God. Still, He was letting me experience His love. I thought, 'Frank Summers, you have nothing at all to commend yourself to God.' Yet, I understood that it did not matter. God was infusing me with peace. The realization of my unworthiness swept over me. Frank the atheist, was being visited by God. The sin of denying God loomed largest of all in my heart. 'Forgive me, God,' I said.

"I remembered the nuns at Mt. Carmel, who taught me that God came as a person. That person was present with me. I was with Jesus. I asked Jesus to save me, please. Immediately, I knew He wanted to save me. I could feel it.

"'What should I do now?' I asked. In an inaudible but clear inner voice, I heard Him say: 'Keep holy the Lord's Day.'

"I was so saddened to acknowledge that for ten years, I had ignored the Lord's Day. I knew I needed to go to Mass and communion, but I realized I needed to go to confession first. Even though it was late, I called Father Martin at Saint Mary Magdalen church. I told him I wanted to go to confession and he said, 'Sure, Frank, come over. I'll be waiting.'

"I told Father that I had not been to confession in ten years. He did not even seem shocked when I told him that I had been denying the existence of God.

"'God forgives even the arrogant,' Father Martin said. 'The important thing is that you are here now.'"

When Frank shared the burden of our troubled marriage, Father said, "Frank, if you put Jesus at the center of your life, He will save your marriage."

On that August night, I sat there next to my husband in our bedroom, overwhelmed by the enormity of Frank's metamorphosis. We talked into the night. We both agreed to stay home from work the following day and continue our dialogue. At first I was skeptical until the next afternoon, when I too heard the voice within.

"Genie, this is not the end of your marriage," I felt Jesus say so very clearly. "This is the beginning!" I felt a sense of freedom burst forth like a geyser. I turned to Frank, our eyes met, we kissed. We laughed for joy. Like a pair of reunited lovers, we embraced.

"Let's really start over," I said. "I'll go to confession, too." A peace came upon us. The storm had passed. We could feel the wonderful presence of God, delivering us from the monstrous evil that had strangled our lives.

The next day, I went to confession and asked Father Martin if we could renew our marriage vows that afternoon. He consented gladly. Frank arrived at the church with a single red rose. Beau witnessed our beautiful ceremony and we experienced the tangible love of God. It was August 15, 1973—the feast of the Assumption—a Holy Day.

Frank's story:

On the night of my conversion and confession, I felt spiritually refreshed, as if I had just taken a shower after ten years of not bathing. Genie and I began to live fully our Catholic faith and our new life in Christ.

For the next two years, it seemed even the mundane, everyday problems of life escaped us. We were lifted up by the grace of God. I believe that God shielded us from problems while we grew strong and able. Genie and I did not return to the love of our honeymoon. Instead, we found a better love, deeper and richer than anything we had previously known.

Through prayer and reading the word of God, our lives changed dramatically. The Lord was setting us free to change our hearts and attitudes, starting with things like giving up smoking and excessive drinking, then moving to areas like attending Sunday Mass and tithing.

Two months after our conversion, we were reading Ephesians 5. God tells husbands and wives to submit to one another. Wives are to be submissive to their husbands and husbands are to love their wives enough to lay down their lives for them. Genie's past women's liberation views made this Scriptural teaching on the role of men and women in marriage difficult to accept. She wondered if there was a more modern interpretation of those Scriptures. When she talked to a priest about it, he told her that the words in Ephesians are for today and forever. He explained that God knows marriages and He knows how they work best. The priest said, "I am counseling lots of couples. The ones that try to live God's Word are experiencing the healing of their hearts."

Genie said, "As Father shared this truth so convincingly, I felt the Holy Spirit's presence. This teaching is God's plan.

I felt like another chain in my life was released." In one area after another, the Lord was setting us free to change our hearts and trust Him in everything.

We wanted our lives, our plans, and our futures to be in His hands. Genie and I began to feel that He was calling us to something more. In gratitude to Jesus for the new life He offered us, we offered Him our lives in service to His Gospel. One day, while at work, I prayed and felt the Lord was saying, "Sell all you have and give alms to the poor, then come follow me."

After a few weeks of dialogue and prayer, we decided to sell everything we had, give to the poor, and live in a small tenant house on my parents' farm. We were blessed by owning only the bare necessities. Such a dramatic step did not happen easily. His drastic leading to this radical change was a surprise and a challenge. Neither of us was sure where this would ultimately lead. It was not easy to part with all our furnishings and cherished possessions. There were tears and appeals to the Holy Spirit for the strength to truly surrender to His Lordship. We were eventually able to peacefully follow God's calling for us.

Although many of our family and friends had long prayed for us, they were taken aback when they learned of our new lifestyle. But "selling all" turned out to be only the beginning. A year-and-a-half after our conversion, we prayed: "Lord if there is anything else you want us to do, we want to do it." At that point I had a vision in prayer and saw myself serving in foreign cultures as a missionary among the poor. We knew this was what God was calling us to do.

For the next twenty-four years, we served as missionaries, beginning with the Tonga Islands in the South Pacific, then American Samoa, New Zealand, Australia, Micronesia,

Latin America, Asia, the Caribbean, the Philippines, and other countries. Genie, Beau, and I served God by spreading the Good News of Jesus. We began as school teachers, but quickly realized that our real ministry was as lay Catholic missionary evangelists.

Not long after arriving in the Tonga Islands, we came to understand Pope Paul VI's encyclical, *Humanae Vitae,* which explains why artificial contraception interferes with the Lord's plan for marriage and family life. The truth and beauty of this teaching opened our lives to all that God had to give us. The result was a purer, deeper love in our intimate life. When Beau was eleven years old, our daughter, Sarah, was born. In the following years, Genie and I had five more children. Initially, we thought having more children meant we had to give up missionary work. But when I looked around me in Pago Pago, I realized that it was not uncommon for the native families to have as many as twelve children. It stood to reason that missionary families with multiple children should likewise be able to live in developing nations.

People wonder how we managed financially through the years. My family has equity interest in oil and gas production, which sometimes paid out royalty checks from fifty to a thousand dollars a month. Primarily, though, we trusted in God's providence for our care and guidance. Financial help often came in the most unexpected ways and when we needed it most.

As the years passed, my parents came to realize this was not just a phase we were going through. Mom had worried, believing that we were living in danger. Dad was convinced that between home-schooling his grandchildren and raising them in third-world countries, I was ruining their lives. Then, one week in the late 1980s, they surprised us and showed up in Mexico where we were serving. They joined us for a week of mission life. They met the local people and joined us for prayer and songs at one of the village communion services. Afterwards, Dad looked at me with tears in his eyes and said, "Now I understand."

To be honest, I had no idea how my kids would do when it came time for college. All I knew was that Scripture tells us God is the source of all wisdom and understanding. I had faith that if God wanted us to be missionaries, our job was simply to follow and trust in His divine providence for our children's higher education. Simon-Peter, our special-needs child, completed a high-school equivalency course. All of our other children have gone to college on full scholarships. They have all distinguished themselves with academic honors from their respective universities. God has provided, full measure. Beau, now forty, teaches at a university in China. Sarah and her kids are full-time missionaries in Mexico. Susanna and her family served for six years in mission and now live a dedicated Catholic life stateside. Mary Magdalen and her family minister to young couples and families. Simon-Peter works in a sheltered employment enterprise. Joseph and John Paul continue missions whenever possible and are university students who engage enthusiastically in evangelism and music ministry.

In 1995, we returned to the United States and I returned to practicing law after a twenty-year absence. Within two years we formed the Family Missions Company. The company assists Catholic laity and families who feel called to foreign mission life. We provide teaching, spiritual formation, and community life. We help the aspiring missionaries raise support and then place them in mission service. We send them out in the name of Jesus. Thus far, we have placed scores of missionaries in long-term assignments and close to two thousand for shorter commitments.

As I reflect on the way God intervened in such an amazing way to save our marriage, I consider how it has fared over the years. Genie and I enjoyed a spiritual honeymoon of sorts that lasted for several years after that wonderful Feast of the Assumption when we renewed our wedding vows. But, as our lives and service to the Lord wore on, we often carried the weight of the cross in our relationship and in family crises. However, by then we had grown strong enough to unite our sufferings and hardships with the sufferings of Jesus. Missionary work brings many difficulties, but it was the best life for us, the one to which the Lord called us. Through it all our marriage has not just endured, it has flourished. The love we knew as newlyweds deepened and broadened after our salvation experience. It has been such a blessing to serve God and to do it together as a married couple. If the Lord calls you into His service, don't hesitate to trade earthly treasures for the heavenly ones.

—Frank and Genie Summers

Frank and Genie Summers *have an international speaking ministry and are also the founders of the Family Missions Company. They may be contacted at home (337) 893-1440, at the Family Missions Company (337) 893-6111, or by writing to 12636 Everglade Road, Abbeville, LA 70510. For more information, visit their website, fmcmissions.com, or email Genie at praisingcajun@yahoo.com*

10

The Power of Forgiveness

With her husband, Steve, sitting beside her in church, Rebecca gazed upon a beautiful marriage ceremony. It made her cringe. An aura of love and joy surrounded the young couple as they made their sacramental vows to one another. Rebecca looked over at Steve, who smiled gently. "I love him so much," she thought. Then her guilt-ridden insides sickened her. "I don't deserve him," she thought. "He wouldn't love me if he knew..."

Many months earlier Rebecca had engaged in an extramarital affair. She was intelligent, ambitious, beautiful, and a well-known news anchor for a television station in a large Midwestern city. She seemed to have it all and yet, in her own home, she felt she had nothing. Her marriage to Steve had become dead at best and wrought with anger and bitterness at worst. Initially, the affair seemed harmless, almost expected in the circles she worked in. Yet, when it was all over, Rebecca could not shake the suffocating guilt. *How could I have been so stupid?* she thought over and over again.

As the bride and groom walked hand-in-hand down the aisle, Rebecca flashed back to her own wedding. She remembered looking into Steve's eyes with love and promising to love and honor him through good times and bad.

They had met on a blind date shortly after college. Rebecca had just started her career as a news reporter at a small-town radio station, and Steve was working as an engineer for a large firm.

They hit it off right away. At the time, their differences seemed to complement each other. Rebecca was emotional; Steve logical. She was a doer and Steve an analyzer. In college, Steve was studious and Rebecca spent most of her time hanging out at the campus radio station.

Rebecca was attracted to Steve's quiet, gentle nature and Steve was immediately drawn to Rebecca's outgoing, fun-loving personality. Although he was usually reserved, Rebecca had a knack for putting him at ease. Love blossomed and they married two-and-a-half years after their first date.

As newlyweds, Steve and Rebecca did everything together, even going to church occasionally. Attending church seemed like a good thing to do every now and then, but it was not a priority. At that time, God was relegated to the sidelines in the game of life. If someone was seriously ill, they might be inclined to send up a prayer, but otherwise, there was no direct communication with Him. Things were going well for them and God did not appear to be very necessary in their lives.

Steve and Rebecca both experienced success at their jobs. Promotions and advancements followed quickly. Seven years into their marriage, they took a second honeymoon in northern Michigan to bask in the glow of their "perfect" marriage. The future looked bright. Steve had just been promoted to chief electrical engineer at his firm. And, after years of working as a radio newswoman, Rebecca had landed her dream job as a television reporter. They had arrived.

But while sailing smoothly into success, Steve and Rebecca failed to recognize the warning signs of a storm in the offing. First, drifting began. The two were ambitious and made work a priority. Marriage, they assumed, would take care of itself. After all, they had done fine for seven years. Rebecca's TV station was pleased with her work and approached her about becoming a night reporter. This meant the opportunity to anchor the news occasionally and also report live five nights a week, a big promotion in the news business. But success came at a price. Rebecca worked a three-to-midnight schedule while Steve worked eight-to-five. And Steve, wanting to live up to his new promotion, eagerly put in extra hours and worked many Saturdays. Married life often boiled down to Sundays.

As their careers and incomes blossomed, their relationship withered. Work consumed them and communication died. Soon they were textbook examples of what marriage experts call "married singles." With the flames of their once-passionate love reduced to embers, the differences that they once delighted in became irritations and sources of conflict. Ugly, vicious arguments flared up over petty things. Sometimes they would brood for a week before making up.

At this point, Steve and Rebecca just pushed ahead over the choppy waters of their marriage. *What other choice was there?* they wondered. Having both come from strong, intact Catholic families, they never seriously considered divorce.

The couple soon bought their first home, which seemed like the next logical step in their marriage. Both hoped that owning a home and spending time together doing home improvement projects would help their relationship. As an engineer, Steve thrived on planning and organization. He felt he was expressing his love for Rebecca by working around the house. In his mind, getting things done and improving the house reflected his commitment to the marriage. But Rebecca craved words of affirmation, physical affection, and a show of love through things like gifts and cards. On weekends, Steve had his "to do" list ready, but Rebecca was not on it. Rebecca, on the other hand, wanted weekends to be their special time together but it seemed Steve just wanted to keep busy with numerous projects. Their bickering increased as the two resented each other for not meeting their needs.

Often, while Steve sat alone in their empty house, he would think, "I'm losing her." It hurt. When Rebecca got home at midnight he was already fast asleep. There was no one to talk to, no one there share a triumph with or offer support. In spite of all their arguments, both felt a crushing loneliness for the other. They missed the love and the laughter. Rebecca and Steve wanted to get back to the happier times, but neither knew the way.

Rebecca and Steve became strangers under the same roof. At this time, their first lifeboat came onto the scene at a most unexpected time and place—a professional basketball game. Rebecca's boss at the TV station was married to an evangelical Christian, Bob, who was on fire with a commitment to Christ.

Rebecca felt it would be a missed opportunity not to accept her boss' invitation. Steve was reluctant at first, but he decided he could at least forget his troubles for a few hours and enjoy the front-row, courtside seats.

Bob sat next to Steve at the game. Before Steve knew what hit him, Bob got him to agree to enroll in a men's Bible study. Steve had never spent much time with a Bible, but in his loneliness and desperation, and in response to Bob's own enthusiasm, Steve felt a glimmer of hope. Maybe this was a place to go for answers, he thought.

The first night, Steve found a seat among the other men. Since this was all new to him, he felt just a little awkward at first. Yet, a warm assurance flowed through him as he opened his Bible. The word of God and the fellowship of other Christian men brought Steve comfort. Most importantly, once he began to seek Christ, he found Him. God's love and teachings began to fill Steve with a newfound love. The shallow faith he had been practicing took on new meaning and purpose as he began to develop a relationship with Christ.

Rebecca could plainly see a difference in her husband, but she was not at all comfortable with it. Since she was not motivated to practice her own faith, being around Steve's enthusiasm for Jesus drove them further apart. Steve longed to share his faith with Rebecca but she felt he was going off the deep end and becoming a wild-eyed fanatic. Rebecca began to question if she even loved him anymore. The magic was long gone and it did not seem he was the man she married. And Rebecca sure did not bargain for a Bible thumper when she said "I do."

Rebecca threw herself into work, putting in long hours and accepting many invitations to public events. At one fundraising event, she ran into a prominent businessman whom she had met on a previous news story. This man had contacts with a number of big stories that Rebecca was working on. They made plans to get together for lunch. *Just business,* she reassured herself. There were phone calls and another meeting. The relationship quickly lost its "business" edge and turned into a physical and emotional attraction. Rebecca enjoyed his compliments and appreciative glances. He was wealthy, powerful and, unlike Steve, he expressed glowing appreciation for Rebecca. There was an electrical charge between them.

You're playing with fire, Rebecca thought after agreeing to a clandestine meeting. But her heart had felt dead for so long. It was exciting to be in the company of a high-powered man who was attracted to her. The steps seemed so small—from meetings and compliments to the first steps toward physical intimacy. With God and religion buried too deep to guide her, Rebecca's self-centered desires blinded her to right and wrong. She kept telling herself it was all perfectly innocent, but then easily gave in when the man made his intentions clear. By that time, she would have been hard pressed to describe it as innocent. So instead, Rebecca determined that it was no big deal and completely her own business. She had a long list of reasons why it was right. Even when the man's irate wife called and screamed at Rebecca, she justified the affair. *This isn't the first time he has cheated, so what's she getting so upset about?* Rebecca thought. *She has her beautiful house, children, and everything money can buy so why doesn't she just leave him alone?*

For months, Rebecca numbed her mind to the gravity of her actions. Working among television news personalities was a slice of the Hollywood lifestyle. Affairs and divorce were common, even expected. And yet, she could never fully shake her Catholic upbringing. Deep down, she knew full well that everything about the relationship was wrong and sinful. It was the forbidden fruit.

Steve rarely saw Rebecca, so he suspected nothing. But as the lies and sneaking around mounted, leading a double life became harder for Rebecca to manage. Stress ate away at her. Finally, repeated phone calls from the despairing and angry wife began to turn the affair sour. The whole affair had turned too ugly for Rebecca to continue. And when it was over, she felt spiritually dead. The excitement that had once been addictive turned into a sickening guilt. She felt used and abused. Though she had no relationship with God, Rebecca felt she was on the road to hell.

When the dust of her adultery cleared, Rebecca desperately feared that she would lose Steve if he ever found out. Listening to Steve's talk of Jesus as their Savior, made her sink even lower. *If Steve ever finds out what I've done, he'll want nothing to do with me,* Rebecca believed. *For that matter, why would God want anything more to do with me?* she asked herself. Rebecca felt she had sunk to a level even too low for God to go.

In spite of putting up a wall to keep all Steve's Jesus talk out, Rebecca could not help but notice the changes in him. But the more Steve talked about Jesus, the sicker with guilt Rebecca felt.

It all came to a head on the Saturday night after the wedding they had attended. Steve was irritated with Rebecca's morose mood all night. She had numbed herself with alcohol and refused to dance with him or engage in conversation. In the wee hours of the morning, during a heated argument, Rebecca blurted out a confession.

"What's wrong with you?" Steve yelled.

"It's not you, it's me," Rebecca cried. "I can't go on this way ... I had an affair." She was shocked at the words that had spilled out of her mouth. It was too late to take them back and she didn't really want to. Rebecca was so tired of living a lie. Now, she braced herself for the inevitable; the condemnation, the anger, the insults.

First, there was silence. Steve felt the wind had just been knocked out of him. He paused and looked to the ground. In that moment, like a drowning man whose life flashes before his eyes, Steve's whole marriage flashed before him. He realized he had not been the husband he should have been.

Then, he looked up at Rebecca. Tears welled in his eyes and then poured out. Rebecca was caught off guard. She could see that she had truly hurt Steve deeper than ever before. She expected him to scream and call her horrible names, but instead he was silent. When he finally spoke, the words were not what she expected.

"I forgive you," Steve whispered through his tears. Then, he hugged her.

No demands for Rebecca to pack up and leave, no threats of divorce, no probing questions insisting on gory details. Just "I forgive you."

And yet, his forgiveness brought Rebecca no relief. It was not just that she expected anger, she had wanted it. *How could he forgive me?* Rebecca wondered. *I don't deserve forgiveness and he deserves someone better than me.* She could not bear it.

The next day Rebecca said she needed to get away for a few days to clear her head and figure out if she still wanted to be married. That night, all alone after Rebecca had left, Steve knelt down at the side of his bed for the first time since he was a little boy. He asked Jesus for forgiveness and to come into their lives and save their marriage. All of a sudden, he felt peace.

Although becoming a committed Christian had brought Steve much comfort, it also challenged him. The verse in Romans 3:23, "All have sinned and all fall short of the glory of God," challenged his heart. He realized he was also to blame by becoming cold and indifferent to Rebecca.

Steve had always considered himself a successful, decent guy and he thought Rebecca was lucky to have him. Not until he put Jesus fully into his life, however, did he realize how sinful and utterly helpless he really was without God in his life. Steve came to understand that his marriage was a covenant relationship with Rebecca and the Lord. If God was going to work a miracle in their marriage, then he believed it was up to him to take the first step—to forgive Rebecca as God forgives him through the sacrifice of His Son.

But forgiveness so quickly was something Rebecca was not ready for. She felt hopeless. *Why should Steve waste his life with me?* she wondered. Even after Rebecca went to confession, she could not accept absolution either from God or Steve. She did not understand the totality of God's forgiveness.

Steve convinced Rebecca to start attending Mass again with him. She still loved Steve, but she hated herself and thought even a painful divorce would be easier than self-examination and rebuilding a broken marriage. Steve's initial forgiveness had been easier on him than the months that followed. He began to grow weary of Rebecca's inability to forgive herself. Also, resentment at what she had done would occasionally eat away at him. Some of the worst fights of their marriage occurred during this time. There were ups and downs. Rebecca would be sullen and withdrawn at times and Steve could become impatient and bitter. To Steve, it seemed Rebecca just wanted to wallow in her sin and not move on. For a time, she buried herself in her work as an escape from her conscience and an escape from God. So God had to take away the distractions; she lost her job.

Even though by all measures, Rebecca seemed to be doing extremely well at work, she was suddenly let go. Since stations play the ratings game, superior work was no insurance in a business that is always out looking for a new pretty face. Stunned, Rebecca packed up her belongings in a box and walked out the door. In the brutal world of broadcasting, Rebecca was easily discarded. Rebecca was devastated and angry. Her anger spilled onto Steve. "If God loved me why would He take away the one thing I was good at and had wanted to do since I was in the third grade?" she demanded. *If this was the work of God*, she thought, *then "no thanks."*

Only later did Rebecca realize that this change was the best thing for her and her marriage. There was a hiring freeze at all the news stations, so Rebecca could find no work to escape into. Except for a few freelance projects, Rebecca was unemployed for six months. It was during this period that God started to reveal Himself to her. Rebecca knew that she needed to repent. She also knew deep down that divorce was a cop-out.

So Rebecca finally quit running from God. Emotionally fatigued, she prayed: "OK, God, I really screwed up and I obviously am not handling things very well on my own. If you are real and you are there, please take over. I can't handle it any more. My life is in your hands." The healing had begun.

Through prayer, studying the Bible, and deepening her relationship with Jesus, Rebecca was finally able to believe what the Lord says to the woman caught in adultery in John, chapter 8, verses 10 and 11: "Jesus looked up and said to her, 'Woman, where are they? Has no one condemned you?' She said, 'No one, Lord.' And Jesus said, 'Neither do I condemn you; go, and do not sin again.'"

The healing process was slow but steady. Although Steve and Rebecca expressed forgiveness to each other, their human hearts battled with bitterness and resentment. There would be tremendous highs followed by equally emotional lows. It was truly a struggle but they felt the grace and love of God holding them together. And going forward with Jesus was very different than what they had experienced in the past. Steve and Rebecca began to realize that their habitual disrespectful arguments did not reflect a Christian marriage. There were still arguments, but viciousness and name calling stopped. They also began praying together after a disagreement. If they slipped and let their anger get the better of them, Steve and Rebecca would go to confession together to receive the gift of forgiveness and God's grace to do better.

One of the best steps they felt they took was to attend a Marriage Encounter weekend. During this weekend, Steve discovered something in himself. Although he had forgiven Rebecca and acknowledged his own guilt in the marriage, he had always felt it was more her fault than his. Even if the blame were fifty-one percent hers and forty-nine percent his, Steve believed that he was less to blame. During that weekend, Steve gave up his superiority. It was a breakthrough for him and the two grew more united that weekend. The weekend also helped them put God fully at the center of their marriage and to appreciate His love for them and their love for each other. Rebecca and Steve learned how to really listen and relate to one another in a Christ-like fashion. Reading and studying Scripture became the lifeblood of their relationship. They found a loving and forgiving God who gives joy, comfort, and direction in their lives. As their relationship healed, Rebecca and Steve's love for each other grew stronger than it had been back in the days when they thought they had a "perfect" marriage.

Once Steve and Rebecca felt secure in their renewed relationship, they experienced the desire to reach out to other married couples. They believe that the grace God poured on their marriage was not just for them. Today, the two share their story before large audiences in order to support and encourage other married couples. Rebecca has shared her story on the air on Evangelical and Catholic radio stations. She also speaks before groups on the negative media influence in our culture and what we can do about it.

Looking back at the past ten years, Rebecca marvels at how God ultimately used everything, the good and the bad, to allow her to give glory to Him and help others. She and Steve realize that had they walked away from each other, not only would the devil have won, but they would have missed out on the best that was to come. Without passing through the suffering of their relationship, they never would have reached the resurrection.

—Patti Maguire Armstrong,
Jeff Cavins, and Matthew Pinto

11

Gambling with Love

Shuffling through the mail, Brad Kremmer pulled out several envelopes from credit card companies and ripped them open. His muscles tightened as he skimmed over the new balances. *She's lied again,* Brad realized. His wife, Jennifer, had promised to stop gambling at the casino and going on out-of-control buying sprees. She seemed to understand the seriousness of their mounting debts, and he really believed her when she tearfully promised to quit. Instead, she had gone through at least another two thousand dollars. It would probably amount to even more by the time the other bills rolled in.

"Jennifer," he called angrily to his wife. "You've got to stop. Can't you see we'll end up going bankrupt?"

Jennifer stiffened when she saw Brad's disappointed face and the pile of bills in his hands. Up until that moment, she had always responded with shame and remorse over her gambling and spending addictions. But suddenly, she released her own building tension.

"I'm stuck home all day with nothing to do but take care of Kristin and housework," she yelled. "All you do is complain and treat me like a child. I'm sick of it and I'm sick of you ... I'm leaving!"

"Where are you going?" Brad demanded.

"Out!" Jennifer screamed. "And don't bother to wait up for me."

Brad looked out the window as his wife sped off in the direction of the casino, where so much of his hard-earned money had gone the last couple months. Since the casino closed at 2 a.m. and was an hour away, he knew Jennifer would not be back before 3 a.m.

Dear God, he prayed. *Watch over her. I'll do whatever it takes to help her, but I don't know what to do anymore. Please help us so Kristin and I can have her back the way she was.*

"Daddy," his two-year-old daughter's voice broke his reverie. "Where's mommy?"

"She's taking a little break, Kristin," Brad answered gently picking her up. "Let's get something to eat and then we can go for a walk, OK?"

Brad smiled at his little girl and choked back his tears. There was a time when he and Jennifer delighted together in their daughter. But now, it seemed the only thing that Jennifer cared about was gambling and shopping. It had happened so fast that Brad could not understand it. Ironically, Jennifer's addiction emerged shortly after he began getting serious about his faith.

Brad and Jennifer were only twenty and nineteen when they married on June 27, 1992. A physical attraction sparked immediately when they met and the emotional attraction followed easily. Brad was one of four children from a Catholic family. Jennifer was Catholic, too, but she had been raised as the only child of a single mom. Brad's levelheaded nature and warm affection gave her the sense of security she had missed being cared for by babysitters much of her life. Jennifer's beauty and fun-loving personality were irresistible to Brad. Marriage made Jennifer feel special and more grown up compared to all her single girlfriends. Having a good-looking and attentive husband seemed to erase all the years of not having a father in her life.

Brad started his own graphic arts business and Jennifer had her own shoeshine company. Life was good: independence, business success, love, and plenty of friends and parties. Two years into the marriage, when Jennifer discovered she was pregnant, she realized life was about to get more serious. Yet, in spite of a twinge of fear, excitement over having a baby filled her. Brad was one-hundred percent thrilled.

As her belly grew, Jennifer often daydreamed of rocking her newborn to sleep, all snuggled up in a soft blanket. But when baby Kristin entered the world, jaundice and a difficult time nursing shattered Jennifer's perfect image. This and sleep deprivation brought out Jennifer's low stress threshold and strong-will. Crying and lashing out at Brad became second nature. Initially, Brad's easy-going disposition chalked it up to hormones and lack of sleep. But when it became habitual, he firmly told Jennifer he did not appreciate her treating him that way.

Jennifer loved Brad intensely. She especially loved his calmness and the respect he showed her even when she did not respond in kind. Still, Jennifer had poor self-control when stress mounted, so Brad learned to stay out of her way until she pulled herself back together.

Within a few weeks, Kristin's medical and nursing problems cleared up and Jennifer began to embrace her new role as a mother. Jennifer and Brad agreed that she would stay home to care for the baby. Caring for her little girl filled her with happiness. She marveled that she could be the mother of such a beautiful creation. Jennifer often delighted in buying pretty baby girl things and dressing Kristin up like a little princess. She spent more than she should have, but Brad did not seem to mind too much.

As Kristin went from baby to toddler, life became pretty routine. In February 1996, Brad and Jennifer planned a trip to Disney World for some excitement and to escape the winter doldrums. At nineteen months, Kristin was an easygoing toddler who would surely enjoy the vacation, too. A couple months prior to the trip, Jennifer became determined to shed the forty extra pounds she had picked up since getting pregnant. Wanting quick results in order to fit into her swimsuit, Jennifer went on a starvation diet. Fruit juice, an occasional piece of bread, and the water remaining after she boiled vegetables was her entire intake. She would not even eat the vegetables she had cooked in the water for fear the extra calories would slow down her weight loss.

Stepping on the scale every day brought a thrill as the pounds dropped quickly. Brad was happy to see Jennifer's pleasure at getting her figure back, but it really did not matter much to him otherwise. He loved his wife regardless of her weight. Brad, however, would not have been pleased had he known of Jennifer's starvation techniques. These she concealed from Brad, as well as the fact that she often felt light-headed and unable to concentrate.

The vacation turned out to be the trip of a lifetime. At her new weight, just walking around in shorts and sunning on the beach brought Jennifer extra enjoyment. But when they returned home to their daily routine, life suddenly seemed painfully dull and boring. The thrill of the fast weight-loss was over now, along with the exciting Disney World vacation. Jennifer felt suffocated by the monotony of housework, the lingering winter, and the demands of childcare. It seemed her single friends were all leading exciting lives while she was tied down. Playing house was not fun anymore.

"I need something more in my life," Jennifer announced. "Maybe I should go back to work or school." As usual,

Brad was supportive. Jennifer was not sure what she wanted to do, but restlessness nagged at her. Anything associated with religion also became a bore for her at this time. "I feel like Catholicism was shoved down my throat as a child," she complained to Brad. "I don't know if it's right for me. Let's take a look at some other churches—you know, just to check things out."

Brad had no interest in looking around at different faiths and Jennifer resented that he did not support her interest. He was unmovable; there was no other faith for him but the Catholic Church. "Do what you have to do," he told her, "but I'm not going anywhere." While many of his old friends had started turning to cocaine and dealing drugs, Brad began embracing his faith with a passion, even to the point of attending regular spiritual retreats run by Opus Dei.

His newfound excitement for his faith had a disappointing side, however. He could not share his enthusiasm with Jennifer. She seemed repelled by anything Catholic. Even going to Mass was more than she cared to do. "I'm not feeling well," was often her excuse. "I'll just stay home with Kristin. You go ahead." When Brad prodded her, Jennifer lashed out in anger. "Leave me alone, I don't want to go," she would yell.

At church, Brad resented his family's repeated inquiries as to why Jennifer was absent. "It's her own decision," Brad would defend her. "Religion isn't something you can force on someone." Yet, inside, he was disappointed and concerned for Jennifer's spiritual well-being. He turned to prayer and trusted that God would guide her. Unfortunately, at the time, Jennifer was headed in a completely different direction.

Occasional shopping trips brought Jennifer some relief from her boredom. Buying clothes was fun and it also made her feel good to dress up Kristin or herself in something new.

Getting a sitter and going out with Brad was something else that Jennifer looked forward to. One of her favorite things to do was to go to the casino with Brad and her mother. They would take forty dollars and make an evening out of playing the slot machines and black jack tables.

Jennifer also kept her relationships with all her single friends going by having an occasional night out on the town with them. Brad saw his single friends less and less because most had either moved away or became involved in drugs. He was usually content to stay home and did not mind letting Jennifer have some time away. As Jennifer's restlessness grew, her nights out with the girls also increased. But it was gambling at the casino that was the most fun for her. Before long, Jennifer started going to the casino alone when she could not find someone to go with her.

The intensity of the slot machines—listening to the bells and musical tones while she watched her money add up—was a thrill. Sometimes she drove home feeling euphoric, with a few hundred dollars more than she walked in with. But more often, she had to keep feeding money into the insatiable machines that sucked up her coins. The draining, demanding urge to get ahead again, drove her to push even more money into the slots. Once she got started, she did not want to stop.

The excitement and intensity of gambling made Jennifer feel alive while the dullness of the rest of her life was something just to get through. The only other enjoyment she had at this time was shopping. Previously, Jennifer enjoyed showing Brad her purchases, but now she just slipped them quietly into the closet before he returned from work.

As the bills mounted, Brad took notice. "Jennifer, you can't keep shopping like this ... how many clothes do you and Kristin need?" Although she knew Brad was right, she hated to hear it. He was especially concerned about the cash advances on the credit cards that evaporated into the casino. "Jennifer, your gambling is getting out of hand," he'd say. "You need to stop."

"I'm so sorry," Jennifer would respond tearfully "I know I spent too much. I promise I'll quit." She had every intention of keeping her word at the time, but then the deep craving to release her tension and pull herself out of the doldrums by gambling grew until she could not stand it.

"I need a break," she would say to Brad. "I'm going with some friends to play pool for a couple hours if that's OK with you."

Brad's stomach began to tighten when Jennifer mentioned going out. *Is she really going out with friends or to gamble?* Brad wondered. Initially, he resisted doubting her word. But when the credit card bills kept increasing, it was obvious Jennifer was lying to him. When Brad expressed his suspicion, Jennifer reacted with anger and headed straight for the casino anyway—angry at Brad for questioning her.

"Jennifer, this has to stop," Brad demanded one day after opening the bills. "Our minimum payment is up to $1000 a month. Your gambling is ruining us."

His patience had worn thin and he began raising his voice when confronting Jennifer. Getting yelled at, even a little, was something that Jennifer could not stand. Her reaction was explosive, and sadly, resulted in another trip to the casino. Sometimes, Jennifer would disappear for days at time. There was no longer any trust between them. Jennifer began to lie as easily as she breathed. Brad started checking the car's mileage and doubted Jennifer's every word. Jennifer resented the way Brad treated her now. She refused to address her own behavior and instead began to see Brad as a hindrance to her happiness.

Maybe being married to Brad was not such a good idea anymore, Jennifer began thinking. "Why don't you just leave me now because you are going to eventually," she often taunted him. Jennifer still loved Brad and Kristin very much, but she began to think that she just was not ready to be tied down to such a seemingly dull life.

In contrast, Brad became more committed to his marriage. He hated what was happening, but Brad knew the wedding vows of his sacramental marriage were forever, in good times and in bad. Daily Mass, the Rosary, and more time spent in prayer were his weapons to fight the evil that was tearing apart his family. Yet the bills and the lies kept mounting. By fall, both sides of the family and all Jennifer's friends realized she had a serious problem. Everyone noticed she was more moody and distant in her relationships with others. When even his own mother questioned the wisdom of staying in such a destructive relationship, Brad felt abandoned by everyone but God. He had thought that surely his parents understood the lifelong commitment of a Catholic marriage. *How could they suggest I get out of it?* he wondered despairingly.

During the last week in December, Brad's parents had arranged for everyone on their side of the family to get together for a ski vacation. "I'm not feeling well," Jennifer begged off. "You go ahead and have fun, and I'll see you and Kristin when you get back."

Brad was not comfortable leaving Jennifer, but he could not physically drag her there. Neither did he want to disappoint the rest of his family by not showing up. "OK," Brad said skeptically, "I'll see you in a few days."

Something unexpected caused the vacation to end a day early. Brad was livid when he returned home to an empty house. And yet, it was what he had expected. He took Kristin to his parents' house and then drove to the casino. It was New Year's Eve, ten months since their Disney World vacation.

As his eyes adjusted to the dim lighting, he frantically scanned the crowd for Jennifer's face. What he saw terrified him. It was Jennifer and yet it was not Jennifer. Her zombie-like face was fixated on a gambling machine until she noticed Brad. Then she instantly seethed with anger and hatred at the sight of him.

Something snapped in Brad. He did not want Jennifer coming home anymore; at least not like this. "I cannot take it anymore," he told her. "You need to leave our home."

"Fine," Jennifer responded defiantly, "Then I'll leave."

In spite of kicking Jennifer out of the house, Brad still loved her intensely. It was clear, however, that Jennifer was getting worse instead of better. He would not continue to enable her destructive behavior. That part was over. And Jennifer knew she still loved Brad. It was the responsibility that went along with being a wife and mother that no longer interested her.

Jennifer was too proud to tell family or friends that Brad had kicked her out. She slept in her car for the next two nights and continued to gamble. On the third day, Jennifer won an $8,000 jackpot. She was euphoric. *Now, I'm really free to have fun,* she thought. She got an apartment and happily shopped for all the furnishings. But that night, she ate her dinner in front of a mirror to escape the shadow of loneliness that came with her freedom.

Unfortunately, the loneliness which might have driven Jennifer back to her family was filled the next day by a cunning young woman who preyed on others. Lydia lived in the same apartment complex as Jennifer. She lived with her parents who were raising her out-of-wedlock child. Jennifer and Lydia became fast friends. Soon, Lydia moved in with Jennifer. Since Lydia was underage, Jennifer often agreed to buy her alcohol and also let her use the bedroom when Lydia's male friends spent the night.

Jennifer and Brad maintained regular contact with each other and he kept faithfully praying for her. But by the middle of February, a friend of Jennifer's told him: "Jennifer says she knows you'll take her back anytime she wants, so she's just going to keep having fun as long as she can." At that point, Brad felt he could not let Jennifer walk all over him anymore.

He called a trusted priest who served as his spiritual advisor and understood the situation. "Father, I'm ready to throw in the towel," Brad stated. "Jennifer's just getting worse. How long am I supposed to take this?"

Brad expected the priest to agree that maybe it was time to move on. Instead, Father's response both surprised and comforted him. "You take it forever," he said. A peace and strength filled Brad as he listened: "You are married to Jennifer forever. "

"But what if she ends up divorcing me?" Brad asked.

"Then you go on and raise your daughter without her, but you will still be married to her. You are being crucified like Jesus, and your suffering is being offered up for Jennifer with our Lord. It does not matter how long it goes on, you are saving her soul with our Lord."

Brad suddenly found the strength and determination to stay the course. Father's words laid his responsibility clearly before him and filled him with peace. It was Lent, and Brad consciously accepted the cross he was being asked to carry and united his sufferings to Christ's. Father's straight talk solidified his determination. There would be no quitting now.

Brad's prayers also changed. No longer was he praying and waiting anxiously for Jennifer to return. No more looking for signs of hope. No more impatience for a change. His work and suffering would be offered up for her soul and he would pray for Jennifer now and forever, regardless of what her response to him was. People on the outside who did not understand his faith or value redemptive suffering could not appreciate what seemed to be a hopeless marriage. But Brad now fully understood the complete lifetime commitment he had made to Jennifer before God, and he was determined to keep it.

Shortly afterwards, Jennifer discovered she was pregnant. Like their love for one another, the physical passion had never left their relationship. Neither of them was surprised to learn of the pregnancy. But when Jennifer was just a couple months along, a phone call from a male friend of Jennifer's led Brad to believe that the child was not his. To think that Jennifer dared to be with another man sickened him and filled him with rage. Shaking, he drove Kristin over to his parent's house and then stormed over to Jennifer's apartment.

"How dare you!" he screamed so loud that it cut into his throat. Jennifer was just waking up from a nap. Seeing Brad's fury and hearing him scream terrified her. Through everything, Brad had never done more than raise his voice. "That baby is not mine, you whore! How could you go to bed with another man?"

Jennifer was shocked and indignant. She had never slept with anyone else. Brad's rage ignited her own. "You're crazy!" she yelled back. "You don't know what the hell you're talking about!"

"You're nothing but a damned liar!" Brad hollered, and then ranted and raved at the top of his lungs.

Jennifer grabbed the phone to call 911. She was terrified that Brad had lost control and might hurt her. Brad grabbed the phone out of her hand and yanked it out of the wall. The screaming continued for several minutes until two police officers showed up. A neighbor had called.

Jennifer's hand had been cut when the phone cord scraped past it. Since the police saw blood, they handcuffed Brad. "No, don't arrest him!" Jennifer pleaded. "It was an accident. Brad would never hurt me." Anyone trained in domestic violence knows that typically the abused wife defends her abuser when the police show up. So Jennifer's defense of Brad fell on deaf ears. Brad was charged with domestic violence and taken to jail.

Sitting in a cell among hardened criminals felt surreal to Brad. *How could this be happening?* he thought. He was too exhausted and emotionally numb to care about the sneers and curious looks from the other inmates. Brad pulled out his rosary. *This is the Cross,* he thought, *and I will carry it for Jennifer. In the name of the Father and of the Son...* The next day, his father bailed him out. Brad's family knew things were getting worse, but they also knew there was nothing they could do or say other than to keep praying themselves.

After Brad left in handcuffs, Jennifer went to visit a friend in another town for a couple days. She had to keep running and filling her emptiness rather than face the horror of what she had done to her life. When Jennifer returned to her apartment, there was an eviction notice on the door. February's rent had been three weeks late and the March rent was not paid. The bad news got worse when Jennifer opened her door.

Everything was gone, even down to her underwear. When Jennifer called around trying to find Lydia, she learned that Lydia had left town for a boyfriend in New Mexico. "That's what she usually does when she robs someone blind," an acquaintance told Jennifer.

Jennifer sat in her empty apartment and looked around. Anger was one of the few emotions she would allow herself and now it filled her. Lydia had been playing her for a fool all along! Her determination to press criminal charges against Lydia met with a brick wall. Since it was a roommate situation, the police refused to get involved. "I'll hunt her down myself," Jennifer decided. "She's not going to get away with this."

Coincidentally, Jennifer had recently gotten in contact with an old boyfriend, Steve, who also lived in New Mexico. When she began to question remaining married, Jennifer started thinking about Steve, whom she had once thought she was in love with. He had been the one to end the relationship over a misunderstanding. Since he was recently divorced, Jennifer began to imagine getting back together with him.

Going to New Mexico to track down Lydia and see Steve would kill two birds with one stone, Jennifer determined. She drove through the night only stopping at a truck stop to sleep in her car for three hours. Then, she drove through the day arriving late in the afternoon. Jennifer called Steve, who agreed to meet her at a bar.

"Hi," Jennifer smiled, walking up to Steve's table. The two talked for a couple hours as if they were picking up from where they left off a few years earlier. Steve had gained weight and did not have the same physical appeal Jennifer remembered, but she had convinced herself even before walking in the door, that this would be some kind of dramatic reunion of two lovers. Jennifer was ready to drop everything if Steve would have her. After all, she decided, there was nothing else to go back to.

Steve listened patiently as Jennifer confessed her troubles to him. His response to her did not fit the script she had written in her head. Although he was divorced and lonely, he would not take advantage of the situation. "You need to get your butt back home and save your marriage," Steve said. "You would be insane to leave your husband. Why would you want to leave a man who has stuck by you through all this? You don't know how good you have it." Hearing these words spoken by an old boyfriend who had nothing to gain by saying them was like a slap in the face. It was more than a rejection; it was an injection of reality.

Steve did not want her. And, Jennifer suddenly realized, she did not want him. She did not even know Steve anymore and here she was ready to leave everything for him. It was as if the cloud of insanity that had covered her had begun to lift. Hearing Steve tell her what an incredible husband she had forced her to face the hell and humiliation she had put Brad through during the past year. And somehow, even though she did not deserve it, he still loved her.

Sitting across from Steve, everything began to sink in—her selfish lifestyle, the betrayal and robbery by a back-stabbing friend, the guilt for abandoning her daughter and husband, and the lack of sleep from her drive. Jennifer finally crumbled. It was time to stop running. The attraction of the single life, spending sprees, and gambling became intensely hollow. Brad and Kristin were the real treasures. She was totally exhausted, both physically and emotionally. Steve let her sleep on his couch a couple nights then gave her gas money for food and to get back home.

Jennifer gave up on trying to find Lydia, whom she heard through the grapevine was in jail. Getting revenge no longer seemed important. Saving her marriage was what mattered now.

It was a very different Jennifer who drove back home. Her heart throbbed with love for Brad and Kristin. She cried for the mistreatment she had inflicted on them. And she did something she had never really done before. She prayed. There was no example of prayer in her home while growing up, with the exception of a few rare blessings before special dinners. But now, Jennifer poured her heart out to God. *Lord, I'll do anything if you give me my family back. Please let Brad still love me. Please help us recover from all the damage I've done.*

Jennifer expected that she would have to work hard to get Brad to accept her back. She trusted that he would still love her and knew he would want them to raise their children together, but she did not imagine that he could easily forget the hell she put him through. When she was halfway home, she called him at work. "Brad," she said nervously. "I'm coming home. I'm so sorry for everything that has happened. I want us to be together again."

Brad was quiet a moment. "Well," he said flatly, "We'll see." He wanted to believe in Jennifer, but she had disappointed him so many times before. Regardless, he would forgive her and welcome her back, convinced that he would stay the course with her no matter what the future held. He put down the phone and prayed.

Jennifer got back into the car and began pleading with God again. *Please let me have my life back again. I want to be a good Christian wife and mother. Help me to be the person you want me to be, Lord.*

Brad looked up from his desk when Jennifer nervously opened the door and walked in. She looked like a scared kitten. He walked over to her and they embraced. "Can you take me back," she cried, melting into his arms. "I do want to be with you for the rest of my life. I'm so sorry for all the things I've done to hurt you."

"Yes, I'll take you back," Brad said through tears of joy. "I love you."

Jennifer moved back that day. Kristin squealed with delight when she saw her. "Mommy's back," she announced.

"I love you so much," Jennifer said, hugging her little girl. "I'm sorry I've been gone so long. But I'm back now forever." During the three months Jennifer moved out, she still spent time with Kristin but her daughter made it clear that she missed having her mommy at home.

Brad expected that there would be an adjustment for Jennifer, but amazingly, they were able to pick up where they left off—only better. Waking up in her own home with her family made Jennifer feel like the luckiest person in the world. She had expected that she would need to work hard to prove herself, but Brad made it clear that he had forgiven everything and would love her for the rest of her life.

The week after Jennifer returned was Easter. Sitting at Mass, surrounded by family, tears of gratefulness filled her eyes. Jennifer truly rejoiced that Jesus Christ had risen that day because now she had risen, too—from being dead spiritually. The following weekend, Jennifer attended a women's retreat. She felt deeply embraced by God's love and forgiveness as she spent the time praying, listening to speakers, and going to confession. For Jennifer, Brad's unconditional love brought her part of the way, then God took over. The desire to read the Bible and pray daily blossomed in her. Listening to speakers talk about God sanctifying us through our daily life brought the deeper meaning she had been searching for. Realizing that God was giving her another baby also filled her with gratitude and a desire to live in union with Him. Jennifer felt overwhelmingly blessed when she reflected on her life; all the people who had prayed for her, her motherhood, and Brad—a virtual hero in her eyes.

After the retreat, Brad noticed a remarkable difference in Jennifer. She was more peaceful and confident in her faith than he had ever seen her. It seemed as if she actually glowed with joy. Now, Jennifer was finally able to share Brad's enthusiasm for his Catholic faith.

Six months after her return, Jennifer gave birth to another beautiful baby girl. That same month, the couple realized they could no longer keep up with their minimum $1,200 a month credit card payments. They declared bankruptcy. It was an unfortunate consequence of Jennifer's past. But instead of lamenting it, it was a reminder to them that they now had so much to rejoice in.

Brad admits that there were many times when the past threatened to haunt them. It would be a passing thought, or the temptation to feel resentment that they had to pay a higher interest rate than people with good credit. For Jennifer, the temptation was to feel bad about herself—how could she have done all that to her daughter and husband? Even though she trusted Brad's forgiveness, a memory would come up and it would hurt. She was ready to move on, but sometimes she feared failing again. But both Jennifer and Brad understood the need to access their marital grace by running to God when thoughts turned negative.

"If these thoughts popped into my head," says Brad, "The only way I could deal with it was to remember the cross. I would give it to our Lord and ask Him to take it away. We need to ask for the superhuman ability to forgive, even ourselves, because it's too big for mere humans. The only way I made it through was by staying as close to God as I could."

Five years after coming back home, Jennifer went into a casino with Brad. She was appalled to the point of feeling nauseous by the emptiness she felt watching people frantically gamble. "I knew they were like I had been," says Jennifer, "trying to fill the hole in their lives with gambling. I wished I could tell them that if they put God in that hole, it would overflow forever and never be empty. Putting time in with God pays you back. Gambling never will."

And when it comes to shopping, Jennifer says it's just a chore now. She buys what she needs and then gets out. There is no longer a desire to spend money for frivolous things.

One of the consequences of Brad's commitment to his marriage vows is the effect it has had on others around him. He says his mother had reached the point where she thought Brad should leave Jennifer. She saw the pain her son and granddaughter were suffering and thought it would be better for Brad to simply end the marriage. Now, however, she acknowledges that their experience made her realize what unconditional love really means. Brad has also spoken to engaged couples and one-on-one with men struggling in marriages. He challenges them to understand that true love means being willing to take up your cross, forget about yourself and to love our Lord no matter what comes. "Marriage is not a 50/50 proposition," he explains. "You need to be willing to give 110 percent."

It has been eight years since Jennifer returned home. She and Brad now have five children, ranging in age from eleven to one. She finds raising her family anything but mundane. Although she has hobbies and a part-time job, she says it is God and her family that fulfill her. She looks at her life in a completely different way now. Instead of looking for fulfillment outside, she finds it through her relationship with God. It is this relationship that helps her see raising her beloved children as a blessing and one of life's true treasures.

As Brad and Jennifer look back over the difficult times and the healing, both say that the love they share now is deeper than anything they ever imagined on their wedding day. "It feels as if there was an overall purification for both of us," says Brad. "It did not come easy, but God was with us and gave us the grace we needed to persevere."

—Patti Maguire Armstrong,
Jeff Cavins, and Matthew Pinto

12
Money Can't Buy Me Love

Mark and Lisa sat at their dining room table across from Linda, the wife of one of Mark's best friends. Both looked expectantly at Linda who had stopped by stating she had something important to share with them.

Looking Lisa square in the eyes, Linda dropped a bombshell. "So, how long have you been having an affair with my husband?"

Lisa gasped. She thought they had been so discreet. "I don't know what you are talking about," Lisa lied. Her hands shook as she brushed a strand of hair from her face, trying to appear nonchalant.

"I know exactly what's been going on," Linda accused. Her angry stare seemed to bore a hole through Lisa. Lisa looked over at Mark who also leveled an unwavering gaze. Like an animal caught in a trap, Lisa felt backed into a corner. There was no escape.

"I'm so sorry," she whispered, then looked to the floor and shuddered. It was the confirmation Linda was looking for. "How could you?" Linda screamed. "I trusted you!" For the next several minutes, Linda unleashed her fury, betrayal, and disgust. Lisa said nothing in her defense. Self-loathing filled every fiber of her being. If the earth could swallow her up, she would have gladly succumbed.

After Linda had exhausted herself, she stormed out. Mark looked over at Lisa who was still shaking. He wondered, *How could she—the mother of our two children—*

have stooped so low? She never seemed to have time for him but she found time to have an affair? "How could you?" he asked disgustedly. "And with a friend of mine?" Then he picked up where Linda had left off, with cutting insults and expressions of disbelief. But as his own anger slowed to a simmer, guilt rose within him.

Mark was quiet just a moment. "There's something I need to tell you," he admitted quietly. "I ... I've had an affair, too."

Lisa was dumbfounded. Suddenly the tables turned. Looking up at Mark, her humiliation gave way to anger and jealousy. *How dare he?* Lisa thought. *Wasn't she the neglected spouse in need of attention?* While she knocked herself out to look good for Mark, he never even seemed to notice. The long hours and big paychecks she brought home was to better their lives. Lisa was outraged. How dare Mark turn to another woman! And how dare he act so indignant towards her!

It was a horrifying moment of truth for Mark and Lisa as to just how far they had grown from each other. As the years passed since their wedding day nine years earlier, they expected their love and happiness to have increased. After all, they had gone from barely making it from paycheck to paycheck to having all the luxuries money could buy. And yet, their marriage was bankrupt. It actually seemed that the harder they both worked to make their lives better, the worse their marriage became. Why couldn't they recapture the love of their early years together; a time when it seemed love was *all* they had?

Mark was a junior on a basketball scholarship at a college in Arizona when he first met Lisa. Sitting in the school cafeteria one day, a good friend of his was raving about her new roommate. "You've just got to meet her," she told Mark. "I think you two would really hit it off."

Just then, Mark's eyes wandered outside the cafeteria window. He noticed a beautiful blonde walking up the steps. "Wow," he thought to himself. "If the roommate looks anything like her, then we *would* hit it off."

Mark was amazed when the blonde walked right up to table he was sitting at. "Mark, I want you to meet my roommate, Lisa," his friend announced.

His heart skipped a beat. She was just as beautiful close up. By the weekend, Lisa had accepted an invitation to attend a party with Mark. The entire time, Mark and Lisa sat outside the party engrossed in conversation with each other. Lisa had never been so comfortable with a man before. As the night was winding down, Mark was surprised by how quickly he had become infatuated with Lisa. He took a chain from around his neck on which hung a silver heart. Placing it around her neck he told her: "Whenever you grow tired of me, you can give this back."

A warm rush of emotion flowed through Lisa. Fingering the heart, she smiled at Mark. "Well, I think I'm going to wear this heart forever because you are the type of guy I would marry." Lisa was caught equally by surprise by the sudden rush of emotion she felt for Mark. She was especially surprised because she had a boyfriend at another college. From that night on, though, Lisa thought only of Mark.

Their love for one another grew fast and furious. By spring of 1983, six months after they met, they were engaged. Mark's family was concerned at first. Since Mark is black, his mother wondered if perhaps a string of unsatisfactory relationships with black women had turned him away from his own race. Lisa's parents were less concerned about the interracial relationship than with her youth. They thought nineteen was too young to make a lifetime commitment. But

Mark and Lisa were convinced that their love was deeply spiritual, that it rose above issues of race or age.

Mark graduated in December 1985, and joined the Navy soon after. Lisa left college to be with him. Once the families realized the two were determined to marry, they gave the couple their blessing. Mark and Lisa were married in the Catholic Church, the shared faith of both families. At this time, neither was really practicing their faith nor did they even know much about it. But because Lisa's parents were so devout, she always made an effort around them to at least appear to be a faithful Catholic. She tried to hide the fact that she and Mark were living together before marriage. Once her parents figured it out, they agreed that the sooner the young couple married, the better, so they would no longer be living in sin.

Deeply in love, every aspect of their life seemed blessed. Regardless of whether Mark had a good or bad day at work, his spirit soared as he drove home. Without fail, Lisa was always waiting to shower him with love and attention. It might be a cold beer and a warm embrace or a candle-lit dinner or any number of little surprises.

Their happiness was based solely on the love they shared for each other. Since their savings account often held only the minimum until the next paycheck, they found creative and romantic ways to spend time together such as picnics or sharing a bottle of wine on the patio during a thunderstorm.

Four months after they were married, Lisa became pregnant. In Mark's eyes, the glow of motherhood made Lisa more beautiful with each passing day. And when he finally held his little son, Caleb, Mark thought he would burst with happiness. Lisa also was filled with joy for the little soul born of their love.

If there had been any lingering doubt from the in-laws that this was a match made in heaven it had completely faded by this time. Both families delighted in their precious new grandson and the love Lisa and Mark had for each other. Sixteen months later, their daughter Madeline was born. Mark and Lisa marveled that another little miracle, born of their love, now graced the earth.

The couple had begun attending Sunday Mass regularly, but more out of superstition rather than devotion. It seemed as though life went smoother on the weeks they went to Mass. Likewise, missing Mass seemed to bring trouble during the week. Being around Lisa's parents also influenced them to attend church regularly. But God was far from their heart. He was not much more than a good luck charm.

As a devoted husband, Mark went with Lisa to her post partum appointment after Madeline was born. "How is the happy couple?" the doctor asked. "A little boy and a girl," he smiled. "You have the perfect family. Now is a good time to think about getting 'fixed.'"

Stunned, Mark and Lisa looked at each another. They were totally ignorant about sterilization. "Isn't that what you do to animals?" Mark asked.

When the doctor explained the surgical process of vasectomies for men and tubal ligations for woman, Lisa and Mark were both fascinated. "We'll talk about it and get back to you," Mark promised.

Mark's original desire to have a large family evaporated overnight. "By the time our two kids are out of school, we will only be in our forties," he calculated. "Just think of the freedom. We could travel and live it up. The best part is that while I'm still in the military, it is completely free."

Lisa, still in the recovery stage of her last pregnancy, was captivated with the thought of being "done." With no consideration of the Catholic Church's opinion on the subject, Mark happily underwent a vasectomy when Madeline was six months old. Although Mark and Lisa seemed to be blissfully ignorant of the fact that they had acted against Church teaching, they made a point never to mention it to Lisa's parents. *Why trouble them with something they might not agree with,* Lisa reasoned. But in reality, Lisa's real motive was to present a veneer of perfection to her parents—to have the perfect marriage, be the perfect parents, and even be the perfect Catholics.

Without realizing it at the time, their relationship began to change. Lisa and Mark's social circle consisted of other couples that thought "getting fixed" was the perfect choice for families with two children. Ironically, now that pregnancy was no longer a possibility, Lisa began to lose her physical attraction to Mark to the point she often did not want to be touched. As a busy, working mother of two young children, this did not seem particularly unusual to her at the time. While their sex life began to dwindle, so did their communication. Lisa grew more distant. Mark developed friendships with other women and was often talking on the phone with them when Lisa returned from work. Not wanting to be a nagging wife, Lisa said nothing. *After all,* she thought, *I have a male friend at work that I confide in, so it's no big deal.*

The couple began seeking friendship and comfort outside of the relationship. Mark's group of male friends became like family to him. Growing up, Lisa had never seen her parents argue, so she equated disagreements with a failed marriage. Thus, rather than express the growing resentments, she buried her feelings. The honeymoon was definitely over.

When Mark received a lucrative job offer back in Arizona, they both jumped at it. Maybe getting a fresh start would breathe a little life back into their relationship, they hoped. Mark began making more money than either ever imagined he would. Since they could afford it, Lisa stayed home to care for the children. But soon, the seeds of insecurity and greed were planted.

"How can you stand to sit at home all day?" a friend asked one evening during a barbecue. "It would drive me crazy."

"I don't mind," Lisa offered weakly. But deep down inside, she craved validation. *I'm nothing more than a housewife,* she thought. *I left school for Mark and now all I do is sit at home and take care of kids all day. And Mark does not even seem to appreciate me.*

Not only did Mark not express appreciation anymore, he made no secret of the fact that a pretty face or shapely body was sure to get his attention. Mark thought that admiring other women was completely normal, just something men did. Lisa again stifled her resentment. But she became determined to fight back. She took a job at a health club, and she was in charge of recruiting company memberships for employees. Her success became an aphrodisiac. Not only was she bringing in large commissions, but working out at the gym brought her the male attention she craved. Unfortunately, none of it was from Mark. On the contrary, Mark became threatened by her fanaticism for working out and was often critical. "You spend so much time at the gym and look at how fat your legs still are," he would say.

Financial success afforded them a bigger house on a lake, new cars, and a boat. Happiness, though, eluded them. Their kids were being raised in daycare, and Mark and Lisa became strangers to one another. To the outside world, they appeared incredibly successful and happy. Juggling jobs and kids during the week and putting on an act during weekend socializing with the "in" crowd, convinced everyone that they had a model marriage. To top it off, they faithfully attended Sunday Mass. Lisa even volunteered as a religious education teacher in her daughter's classroom. But the false god of materialism ruled their lives; the real God was given little attention.

In spite of fooling the rest of the world, Mark could not lie to himself. Loneliness nipped at his heels. He tried to express to Lisa that all the money was not bringing them happiness. She reacted bitterly. "What's wrong with you?" she asked. "I thought being successful was a value we shared?" Lisa turned further away from Mark and towards the company of other friendships with men and male business associates. The men knew just how to validate Lisa's craving for male attention. When she brought up a complaint about Mark, they quickly heaped on flattery such as: "If I were your husband, I would never treat you that way," or "I think you have great legs."

Mark's response was identical. Other women provided the attention and comfort he was not getting in his marriage. The game was played the same way: "I would never treat you that way if I were your wife," women would whisper to him.

Both affairs took place around the same time. Since they spent so much time away from home in the company of members of the opposite sex, their schedules were ripe for an affair. In both instances, the affair was more emotional than physical. Self-deception initially blocked any guilt. Thoughts such as: "I'm not hurting anyone, I deserve this, and he/she doesn't care about me anyway," convinced them that breaking their marital vows was no big deal.

Mark ended the affair on his own. Remorse had begun to eat away at him for crossing a line he never thought he would cross. At this point, Lisa was running too fast to feel anything. But when the truth was finally revealed, both felt intense guilt and a deep distrust of the other. The emptiness in their relationship was exposed and festering like an open wound. Both deeply resented the other's actions but felt unable to say much because of their own behavior.

"Well, there's nothing we can do but go on from here," Mark said, without much emotion. They both promised never to stray again. Yet neither felt confident with the other's pledge. *If he/she did it once, what's to prevent it from happening again?* they both wondered.

Mark actually wanted to talk about the situation. "How did we get here?" he wanted to know. But Lisa could not bear to face her own failings head on. Nothing was ever worked out. There were never any fights, but the two became strangers.

Shortly after the affairs came to light, Lisa took a job an hour away. She came home once or twice a week and weekends. Mark was miserable to the point of depression. His work became a burden; he had to force himself to even show up. Lisa saw Mark as weak, as not being the ambitious provider. *Now I have to work harder to make up for him,* she determined. It added a greater strain between them.

"We need to work on our relationship," Mark pleaded. But Lisa put up a wall, unable to face their struggle and the fact that her perfect exterior was a lie. Instead, she reacted by working harder and striving to make more money. The little time Mark and Lisa did spend together was torture. In front of friends, they were the same fun-loving twosome. But at home, both went to extremes to avoid being alone together.

One day, an acquaintance of Mark's showed him a picture that included his old friend, Lisa's college roommate. It suddenly took him back to happier times and stirred a feeling of hope within him. *I don't have to be miserable,* it dawned on him. *We don't have to stay married. I can get out and be happy again.*

With Lisa gone so much, Mark discovered he was capable of managing the house and kids without her. *I don't need her,* he began thinking. *The love is gone and she doesn't want to work on the marriage, so there's no reason to stay.* The thought of divorce buoyed his mood higher than it had been in a long time. Mark was so convinced of the finality of the decision that he called Lisa's brother with the announcement. "We're done," he told him. "I've had enough with your sister." Mark detailed his complaints against Lisa. He even revealed her affair but failed to mention his own.

Lisa was outraged when she learned of Mark's phone call. "How dare you?" she accused Mark. "You had no right to tell my brother anything!" The realization that the darkness had come into the light for all to see, horrified her. "How can I ever face my family again?" she cried. She seethed with resentment at Mark. Yes, she would be more than happy to divorce him.

When Lisa's parents called, she refused to get on the phone. Mark held the phone up to her ear. Reluctantly, she listened. "Lisa," her mom said in a gentle voice, "you don't need any more advice. I just want you to know that we love you and we are going to be praying for you." In spite of the humiliation that filled Lisa, her mother's voice gave her a flicker of comfort. She was going to need prayers as she and Mark ended their ten-year marriage.

Once the families learned of the impending divorce, Mark and Lisa felt it was time to tell their two children ages eight and nine now. "Kids," Mark called. "Come on into the living room. Your mother and I have something to talk to you about."

The kids bounded into the room, expectantly. Lisa and Mark looked at one another, both steeling their emotions. Mark took a deep breath and began: "You know how brothers and sisters fight and don't get along sometimes? Well, sometimes moms and dads don't get along and are not able to work things out. That's the way it is with your mom and me, so we are getting a divorce."

Mark and Lisa were not prepared for their despairing reaction. Caleb and Madeline broke down upon hearing the word "divorce." Their little bodies shook as they hugged each other and sobbed. Lisa and Mark were unsettled by their kids' reaction but they remained unmoved. "It has to be this way," they both agreed. "They will get over it."

But Mark began having second thoughts. He started thinking and looking over the relationship. He wondered, *Do I want to look back one day and say, "what if?" Did we really exhaust every possibility?*

Mark began bringing home marriage books and asked Lisa to read them. She would agree but then never pick them up. Lisa felt numb and blamed Mark for all their unhappiness. *Haven't I been knocking myself out all these years trying to look good for him and work hard for the family? He never appreciates any of it,* she surmised.

And yet, Lisa too began to feel panicked at the finality of divorce. She called their parish priest one day. "Father, we are in trouble and need to see you. We are going to get a divorce. What can you do for us?"

The priest referred Mark and Lisa to a Christian counselor. For $100, the counselor listened to their story and gave his conclusion: "Maybe you were not meant to be together. You'll never get along." It was the confirmation they both felt they needed—the marriage was hopeless. Both felt a sense of peace that no more second guessing about the relationship was necessary. Although in their mind the decision was made, neither made the next move for the next couple months.

Finally, Lisa called and arranged for a visit with a priest they both really admired. Expecting just a social call, the priest's face dropped when he learned of the couple's plan to divorce. They went on to build their case, hoping to gain sympathy and agreement from the priest.

He listened intently and then asked Mark and Lisa a few questions. "Do you know what the Church teaches about marriage? What God's intention is for the marriage covenant? What St. Paul says about marriage?"

Lisa and Mark admitted ignorance. The priest told them they needed to go home and do some studying about marriage before they proceeded any further. Until then, the idea of consulting Scripture or the Church regarding marriage had never occurred to them. It was as if a door they had never thought of suddenly opened.

Mark tackled the priest's assignment with vigor. He went to a Catholic bookstore and bought a large stack of books from the marriage section. At home, he holed up in the bedroom and began reading the Bible. Opening up St. Paul's Letter to the Ephesians, Mark read: "Wives be submissive to your husbands." *Aha,* he thought. *Lisa is not being submissive to my needs. Wait until I show her this.* But then he read on: "Husbands love your wives as Christ loved his church." Mark paused and re-read these words. Christ had died for the Church, he realized.

He went on to the *Catechism of the Catholic Church* and read about God's plan for marriage. Mark was amazed. After eleven years of marriage he was discovering for the first time that marriage was supposed to be a holy and sacred covenant and that it was his spiritual duty to love and protect his wife and the relationship. Mark continued on with the early Church fathers and the various encyclicals, particularly John Paul II's *Familiaris Consortio* (On the Family). After a two-day odyssey of intense reading, Mark called Lisa into the room.   "Look what our Church has to teach about marriage," he said and began reading some of the passages he had highlighted. "We are not even coming close to it. What were we thinking?"

As Mark read, Lisa felt a fire ignite in her heart. For so long she had shut her feelings off, convincing herself they were not in love anymore. Now, listening to Mark's impassioned voice, she saw him through different eyes and was hungry to hear more. Then Mark suddenly stopped, and looked into Lisa's eyes. He took her hands in his and began to pray. "God, we tried to live our relationship the way we thought we should and it did not work. We tried to live our life the way society tells us to and it didn't work. Heavenly Father, please come into our lives and show us how you want us to live this thing called marriage. And if you deliver us from this evil, we will spend the rest of our lives working to help other married couples in trouble." It was the first time the two had ever prayed together. Mark thought, *If God can save us, we'll really owe him.* Thus, the promise of helping others popped into his mind as the most appropriate way to thank Him.

Lisa and Mark stayed up until the wee hours that night talking. For the first time in many years, the embers of their love re-ignited. Listening to Mark talk about his desire to be committed to both God and their marriage warmed Lisa's heart. And Mark delighted in Lisa's rapt attention and hunger to hear more.

It started that night, talking about their marriage, but the excitement overflowed into other areas of their faith. Previously, neither had really understood—and certainly not embraced—their Catholic faith. Suddenly every day was a new and exciting day of discovery about their faith and each other. As they began to read and study, it became clear to them how they ended up on a course of destruction. By straying from God, they ended up also straying from each other. Selfishness and materialism had been their driving force instead of love and sacrificial giving to the other.

Both quit their jobs in order to make God and family their number one priority. It seemed a radical move, but now the couple was eating and breathing their Catholic faith and marriage recovery. To support themselves, they were able to do consulting work in sales and marketing. The flexibility allowed them to keep their priorities and continue reading and studying. As they strengthened their relationship with God, their marriage flourished naturally and the graces began to flow. One of the cornerstones of their new life together was to recognize that God must be the rightful authority in their lives, not them. They realized that when they were distant from Him and tried to run their own lives, they lapsed into selfishness and sin. Mark and Lisa now looked to the Church to lead them instead of looking to their own self-will.

Within several months, the incredible healing Mark and Lisa experienced evolved into a desire to save other couples the heartache they had gone through. They talked to people working at the diocese and in marriage ministries and ended up mentoring other couples. Almost immediately, they began receiving referrals and even began to develop long-distance relationships with people. "It's amazing," Lisa marveled upon learning the news. "A year-and-a-half ago we had planned on divorce. Now we are going to help other couples not to get a divorce."

It was at this time that Mark discovered the Church's teaching on contraception and sterilization. Gut-wrenching guilt felt like a punch in the stomach when he realized he had closed himself off to God's life-giving gift of procreation. It was then that Mark looked back and realized that the insidious selfishness that once grew in their marriage had its roots in his vasectomy.

After consulting with a priest, Mark understood that the Church did not require him to have a reversal. He and Lisa continued their new life together and accepted that their ignorance had led them to a bad decision but it was in the past. Then, one summer, Lisa and Mark attended a marriage conference in which the speakers talked on the Church's teachings on sex and marriage. One of the speakers, Christopher West, an author and then-director of the Archdiocese of Denver's marriage and family life office, spoke on *Living the Gift: The Joy of Sacramental Sex*. For an hour Mark and Lisa listened to West explain how we usurp God's power when we take into our own hands the decision of whether or not our lives will be blessed with a child.

The ride home was a quiet one. They had dedicated themselves to helping other couples enrich their married and family life. One of the main goals was to educated people on God's plan for the marriage covenant and make sure that Catholic families understood the teachings of the Catholic Church. Mark felt he could not preach what he was not practicing. Through prayer, he and Lisa agreed that Mark should have his vasectomy reversed even though they did not have the large sum of money it would cost. Still, they felt they needed to proceed and let God work out the details.

Lisa found a doctor who once performed vasectomies until his own conversion convinced him to stop. His practice was now built solely on doing reversals. When Mark and Lisa met with the doctor, both felt a sense of peace and sureness that this was what they needed to do. After setting up an appointment for surgery, Lisa asked if the doctor would agree to setting up some sort of payment plan. The doctor sat back in his chair and looked up at the ceiling for a moment. Then, he slowly leaned forward and said, "I think you two are a wonderful couple, and I like the ministry and the work you want to do. In fact, I like it so much that I'm going to invest in it." He paused and said, "I'll see you next Tuesday and bring $500." Little did he know that was the exact amount they had in savings. Tears of joy and amazement flowed down their cheeks as all three hugged each other.

Not knowing whether the surgery would be a success or if they would ever have the blessing of more children, Mark peacefully lay down on the operating table. "Now, everything is in God's hands," he thought.

Ten months later, Mark and Lisa joyfully welcomed their beautiful daughter, Theresa Ann, into the world. Then, two years later, after one miscarriage, little brother Paul Michael joined the family.

Mark and Lisa went from the brink of divorce to helping other couples. Now that they are living in communion with God, they feel the graces that allow them to live in communion with one another. There are still difficulties and hard times, but the difference is that both have faith that with God they can handle whatever comes their way. They also revel in God's ability to take even their mistakes and use it for His glory. When they talk to other couples in troubled marriages, none can say, "Yeah, but you don't understand." They understand fully that God can change everything, no matter how hopeless things may seem.

The mentoring they have done results in couples attesting to dramatic changes in their relationships as they attempt to live the "gospel of life." Mark and Lisa first encourage couples that they need to take ownership of their faith by getting to *know Christ* and not just know *of* Him.

They have been asked to give workshops and have personally mentored more than one hundred couples. It's often a couple's last hope after counseling has failed. Through mentoring, they walk through life with a couple in many ways. For instance, they've found that a lot of couples find it hard to engage in the most intimate act of all: prayer. They teach partners the importance of praying together and help them develop a sense of comfort by praying with them.

By working with couples, praying with them and for them, and sharing their own experiences, Mark and Lisa say they have known no greater satisfaction in their working life. God has done great things for them and now one of their greatest desires is to share it with others.

—Patti Maguire Armstrong,
Jeff Cavins, and Matthew Pinto

Marriage Renewal Resources

There are two major Catholic marriage renewal organizations in the United States, *Retrouvaille* and *Marriage Encounter*. Both offer many helpful resources, including weekend programs.

Retrouvaille

The following mission statement is from the official Retrouvaille website:

> "Retrouvaille is a live-in weekend and post-weekend program for married couples. The emphasis is on a technique of communication between a husband and wife. During the weekend, a series of in-depth presentations are given to you and other couples like yourselves. Each presentation, given by one of three married couples and a priest, focuses on a specific area of a marriage relationship. After each presentation, you will have a chance to reflect on it by yourself, and then discuss it with your spouse in complete privacy. The weekend is not a spiritual retreat, not a sensitivity group, not a seminar, nor is it a social gathering. You will, however be encouraged, to put the past behind you and start 'rediscovering' one another again. The weekend is not a 'miracle cure.' Therefore, post-weekend sessions have been designed to continue the marriage renewal begun on the weekend. These follow-ups review earlier concepts in greater depth, present new ones, and help you apply these concepts to your own marriage."

For more information, visit www.HelpOurMarriage.com or call 1-800-470-2230

Marriage Encounter

The following information is from the Worldwide
Marriage Encounter website:

> "Marriage Encounter offers a weekend experience
> designed to give married couples the opportunity to learn
> a technique of loving communication that they can use for
> the rest of their lives. It's a chance to look deeply into their
> relationship with each other and with God. It's a time to
> share their feelings, hopes and dreams with each other. The
> emphasis of the Marriage Encounter weekend is on the
> communication between husbands and wives. The weekend
> provides a conducive environment for couples to spend
> time together, away from the distractions and tensions of
> everyday life, while encouraging them to focus on each
> other and their relationship."

For more information, visit www.wwme.org or call
1-800-795-5683

Acknowledgments

Many thanks to:

- All the couples who shared their trials and struggles—and ultimately their joys of renewed love—with us and our readers.

- Tracy Moran for her creative and insightful editorial contributions to many of the stories.

- Our team of reviewers, whose thoughts and insights helped make great stories even better (*listed alphabetically*): Kari Beckman, Lori Boyd, Felicia Coffey, Barbara Cope, Jennifer Cope, Amy Fontecchio, Mary Kate Hayden, Elena (Helen) LaFrance, Ann McCarney, Pinky McGreevey, Elizabeth Moses, Lorraine Parkinson, Lisa Trucksess, John Unger, and Dana Vink.

- Michael Flickinger and Michael Fontecchio for their editorial and technical assistance.

- Kinsey Caruth, our award-winning graphic designer and friend, for another wonderful cover.

— Jeff Cavins, Matthew Pinto, and
Patti Maguire Armstrong

Editor and Contributor Contact Information

To contact one of the contributors, please write them at the following address:

(Name of writer)
c/o Ascension Press
P.O. Box 1990
West Chester, PA 19380

Or by e-mail:
AmazingGrace@ascensionpress.com

To contact one of the co-editors, please write them at one of the following addresses:

Jeff Cavins
P.O. Box 1533
Maple Grove, MN 55311
Or at: jcavins@attbi.com

Matthew Pinto
P.O. Box 1990
West Chester, PA 19380
Or at: mpinto@ascensionpress.com

Patti Maguire Armstrong
P.O. Box 1532
Bismarck, ND 58502
Or at: patti@bis.midco.net

About the Editors

Jeff Cavins served as a Protestant minister for twelve years before returning to the Catholic faith. His story is chronicled in his autobiography, *My Life on the Rock* (Ascension Press). Jeff is best-known as the founding host of the popular EWTN television program "Life on the Rock." With Matthew Pinto, he is the co-creator of the *Amazing Grace* series. Jeff is also the creator and principal author of *The Great Adventure*, a popular Bible study program. His newest book, *I'm Not Being Fed: Discovering the Food that Satisfies the Soul* (Ascension Press), was released in September, 2005. Jeff and his wife, Emily, reside in Minnesota with their three daughters.

Matthew Pinto is the author of the best-selling question-and-answer book *Did Adam & Eve Have Belly Buttons?* (Ascension Press), and is the creator of the *Friendly Defenders Catholic Flash Cards* series. Matt is co-founder of several Catholic organizations, including CatholicExchange.com and Envoy magazine, and the creator, with Jeff Cavins, of the Amazing Grace series. Matt and his wife, Maryanne, live in Pennsylvania with their five sons.

Patti Maguire Armstrong is the mother of eight children. She worked in the fields of social work and public administration before staying home full-time to raise her children. As a freelance writer, Patti has written more than 400 articles for both secular and religious publications. She has authored the book *Catholic Truths* *for Our Children* (www.raisingcatholickids.com) as a guide to help parents pass on the Catholic faith to their children, and served as co-editor of *Amazing Grace for the Catholic Heart* and *Amazing Grace for Mothers.* Patti and her husband, Mark, live in North Dakota, where they home school their children through high school. They are also raising a foster child from Kenya.